SHORT-TERM RENTAL, LONG-TERM WEALTH

SHORT-TERM RENTAL, LONG-TERM WEALTH

Your Guide to Analyzing, Buying, and Managing Vacation Properties

AVERY CARL

BiggerPockets®
PUBLISHING
Denver, Colorado

Short-Term Rental, Long-Term Wealth: Your Guide to Analyzing, Buying, and Managing Vacation Properties
Avery Carl

Published by BiggerPockets Publishing LLC, Denver, CO.
Copyright © 2021 by Avery Carl.
All Rights Reserved.

Publisher's Cataloging-in-Publication Data

Names: Carl, Avery, author.
Title: Short-term rental , long-term wealth : your guide to analyzing , buying , and managing vacation properties (with Airbnb, Vrbo, and more!) / by Avery Carl.
Description: Denver, CO: BiggerPockets Publishing, 2021.
Identifiers: LCCN: 2021935115 | ISBN: 9781947200449 (paperback) | 9781947200456 (ebook)
Subjects: LCSH Vacation rentals. | Vacation homes. | Real estate investment. | Real estate development. | Personal finance. | BISAC BUSINESS & ECONOMICS / Real Estate / General | BUSINESS & ECONOMICS / Real Estate / Buying & Selling Homes | BUSINESS & ECONOMICS / Personal Finance / Investing
Classification: LCC HD7289.2 .C37 2021 | DDC 643.25--dc23

Printed on recycled paper in the United States of America
10 9 8 7 6 5 4 3 2

Dedication

For Luke, thank you for always pushing me to make my dreams a reality, and thank you for everything you do every day to make them come true. Every success we have had is because of you.

For Max and Nash, you can be anything you want to be if you put your mind to it. I can't wait to see what you grow up to become, and I'll have your back every step of the way.

Love, Mama

TABLE OF CONTENTS

Chapter 4
GENERAL STR ANALYSIS

Chapter 5
ANALYZING YOUR POTENTIAL STR PROPERTY

PART 2
SELF-MANAGING YOUR STR REMOTELY

Chapter 6
DO I NEED A PROPERTY MANAGER?

Chapter 11
MANAGING YOUR RENTAL

Chapter 12
BUILDING WEALTH AND SCALING YOUR PORTFOLIO

ACKNOWLEDGMENTS

PART 1
ACQUIRING A PROPERTY

Chapter 1

INTRODUCTION

It's never too late to work 9-5—you can work real hard, or just fantasize.

—KISS, "GOD GAVE ROCK AND ROLL TO YOU II"

When I was a kid, my family would rent a huge beach house for a week-long vacation in Destin, Florida. That's what nearly every family does when they vacation on Florida's Emerald Coast.

Every year, I wondered who owned the houses we rented—they were always huge, with a private pool, right on the beach. I assumed they belonged to some ultra-wealthy person who had endless amounts of disposable cash and spent a few weeks a year at their luxurious beach home. Though I often wondered what they did for a living to be able to own such a property, it never occurred to me that people were actually making money off their beach homes.

Little did I know that one day I would grow up to become one of those financially savvy people.

In this area of Florida, everything from simple one-bedroom condos to luxury twelve-bedroom villas with rooftop pools is available to rent on an overnight or weekly basis. As far back as I can remember, I have never heard of anyone staying in a hotel on the Emerald Coast. My parents' families rented houses for vacation here in the 1960s and '70s, when my folks were kids. My mom and dad even met while renting in the same condo building in Destin.

It didn't dawn on me until well into adulthood that owning this type of rental could be a viable investment strategy, one that might build my personal wealth to an extent I never considered possible.

I was introduced to the idea of short-term rentals as a means to cash flow in my early twenties in New York City. I was living with two room-mates in a 1,000-square-foot apartment in Bushwick, Brooklyn (don't call me a hipster). One roommate's boyfriend lived down the street and was in a band that toured several months a year. While on the road, he would rent out his room to cover his expenses. That strategy worked so well for him that he convinced his roommates to allow him to rent out the couch while they were all home as well, even though they didn't have a true living room. As is common among young, broke New Yorkers, the living room had been walled off to create a private bedroom for one of the full-time roommates. Thus, the couch ended up in the kitchen. The kicker? It wasn't even a real couch; it was a futon, the kind that one can get at Target for $250. Who on earth would want to rent a crappy futon in someone's kitchen?

As it turned out, lots of people were happy to rent a futon in someone's kitchen. The renters were mostly other 20-somethings seeking adventure in New York City on a very modest budget. The roommates rented out that couch in the kitchen often enough to bring in a few hundred bucks a month, which knocked down everyone's rent significantly. This led to the musician renting a handful of long-term furnished apartments in Brooklyn that he in turn rented out by the room on an overnight basis (a practice called rental arbitrage, which has since been heavily regulated and all but outlawed in New York).

He and my roommate were able to spend months at a time living in a beach house in Puerto Rico while I was picking up double shifts as a bar-tender to afford flights home to Mississippi for the holidays. Rather than seeing this system for the genius entrepreneurial venture it was, I saw it as a quick hustle to avoid having a real job. I assumed the opportunity to generate income that way was not sustainable and would dissipate at some point.

Unfortunately, it took several more years before this all made sense to me. My then boyfriend (now husband) Luke and I started our real estate investment journey in 2013. Fresh on the heels of Hurricane Sandy, we decided it was time to move out of New York City to a cheaper and easier place to live: Nashville. (Spoiler alert: Nashville is no longer a cheaper and easier place to live than New York.) My husband is a classic rock and metal DJ on SiriusXM radio, and we chose Nashville because he could easily transfer there from the New York office. In Nashville, we could buy a house to live in, and I could work on my master's degree.

When I did earn my MBA, I earnestly set off down the path of a "real job" that would lead me to a boss I hated and a salary of $35,000 a year. While many of my classmates made deliberate and, quite honestly, obnoxious efforts to network as much as possible in hopes of furthering their careers, a line from one of my favorite movies, *Almost Famous*, continually echoed in my brain: "Don't worry, you'll meet them all again on their long journey to the middle." There I sat in my rolling chair in that open-concept office, eagerly awaiting a promotion that might never come. Sounds like fun, right?

Around that time, as we were looking for a primary home to buy, our real estate agent kept pushing us toward an ultra-hip neighborhood in Nashville that was appreciating at lightning speed. Having come from Brooklyn, we were tired of neighbors and opted to buy a house located on a few acres in the country outside Nashville instead. We didn't know it at the time, but this house would eventually become our first real estate investment as a rental property. However, in the meantime, our minds kept wandering back to those appreciation numbers in the ultra-hip neighborhood.

We had absolutely zero idea what we were doing. We had not educated ourselves about real estate investing—heck, we didn't even know it was called real estate investing. We rolled the dice in April 2016 on a cheap but cute property just outside the ultra-hip neighborhood. Our hope was that one day we could sell it to pay for our future children's college tuition with the appreciated value.

As extreme luck would have it, that property immediately rented for almost $1,000 more than the monthly mortgage payment. (This was well over 1 percent of the total purchase price, the benchmark laid out in the

1 percent rule.) Once we got that first rent check, we were hooked—we knew we wanted to scale our portfolio and turn this into a true business. At that point, we began educating ourselves on real estate investing. We both inhaled every book, podcast, and any other piece of content we could find on the subject. We drove around and looked at real estate in our free time, talked about it over dinner, and texted about it at work. We had been bitten by the real estate investing bug, and we were going to scale this thing into something meaningful for our growing family, no matter what.

Yet there was one major stumbling block: capital. To put it bluntly, we didn't have much. We had worked hard to save enough for a down payment on a second property. (I could go into detail on how we did it, but you'd be better off reading Scott Trench's book *Set for Life*.) If we had only enough capital for one more purchase, we wanted to maximize the return we could squeeze out of this last bit of capital, and buying one more single-family, long-term rental just was not going to get us there fast enough.

On the long drive home from my grandmother's house in the popular vacation destination of Destin, I started perusing properties on my phone in similar vacation markets. I wondered what the cash flow in markets like those would be, and the idea of buying something to rent by the night crossed my mind. After a few minutes, I realized we could make more money from our one little down payment if we could invest it in a short-term rental rather than a long-term one. We decided to look more closely at short-term rentals (or Airbnb properties, in non–real estate investor lingo).

In Nashville, regulations were constantly changing. Although the cash flow was there, the short-term-rental environment was just too unstable for us to feel comfortable dumping the last of our nest egg into that market.

I started zeroing in on properties in the Great Smoky Mountains, just a few hours east of Nashville. When I was a kid, my parents took us on weekend vacations to Pigeon Forge and Gatlinburg on several occasions. For those getaways, we rented a cabin rather than a hotel room. That's what everyone does when they visit the Great Smoky Mountains. Once I realized this, it all finally clicked: I could combine my Brooklyn friend's new-school short-term-rental strategy with the decades-old, tried-and-true short-term vacation rental market of the Great Smoky Mountains.

Rather than rent out a crappy futon in our kitchen, we could rent out a full single-family home to vacationers in a market where renting a privately owned property rather than a hotel had long been the norm for vacationers. Because short-term rentals were old news in this market, there weren't constant clashes among the city council members, hotel lobbyists, disgruntled neighbors, and short-term-rental owners. We didn't have to (and still don't) worry about unfavorable short-term-rental regulations. We had found our rental market.

Luke and I quickly got started looking for properties. We began our search for a local agent to help us, but when we started asking about return on investment, price per night, and occupancy rate, we were continually directed to the website of one of the big local cabin management companies to discuss their management fees. We had no intention of paying the exorbitant fees charged by local managers, so we decided to figure out a way to manage our property on our own, without the use of a property manager. No matter how many agents we called, we could not find one who could answer any questions on return on investment, income and analysis, or how to manage a vacation rental remotely.

We decided to take a swing at a property for which the numbers appeared to work based on our analysis. The only advice we received was from the owner of a neighboring cabin who lived in Memphis and happened to be managing her property from there. We found her on Airbnb, and she graciously agreed to answer our questions on how she was able to do it and what struggles she encountered in "self-managing" a short-term rental from across the state. Armed with a few recommendations from her on how to find a housekeeper and a handyperson, as well as a general description of how things worked, we were off to the races with our first short-term rental.

To make a long story short, we developed our own systems and processes, and five years later, we have scaled our portfolio to about thirty units. Our short-term rentals gross upwards of $400,000 a year, and our long-term rentals gross upwards of $100,000 a year. I got my real estate license in 2017, and I started The Short Term Shop, a real estate firm focused on short-term-rental investing. We now have offices in the Great Smoky Mountains in Tennessee, the Emerald Coast of Florida, the Blue Ridge Mountains in Georgia, and Gulf Shores, Alabama, with more office openings on the way. In addition to working on traditional real estate agent transactional responsibilities, we also work to educate our buyer clients on how to implement the same systems that have made us successful investors in hopes that our experiences can aid them in their journey toward financial independence. I have sold more than $500 million in cash-flowing, short-term rentals since our inception and have trained hundreds of investors on how to manage their short-term rentals no matter where they are in the world (from a tour van to the desk at their "real job"). With the use of a few systems, automations, and apps, they can avoid paying a property manager tens of thousands of dollars a year to do it for them.

In this book, I will teach you the methods that worked for us, including the lessons I learned that got me from one property to a portfolio generating half a million dollars in just five years. You will learn how to choose the most profitable and historically recession-resistant markets for short-term-rental investing, as well as how to choose the properties with the highest return-on-investment (ROI) potential within those markets. You will learn the questions to ask and items to check out before buying, such as state and local short-term-rental regulations and taxes. Plus, I will explain how to analyze potential short-term-rental investment properties and how to manage them from your smartphone, from anywhere, without the use of a property manager, in as little as thirty minutes a week. Before we dive in, let's start with the basics of what a short-term rental is and how to identify a potential investment property.

WHAT EXACTLY *IS* A SHORT-TERM RENTAL?

In real estate investing, a short-term rental (STR), sometimes called a vacation rental, is a property that is rented out to guests on an overnight basis rather than with a monthly or annual lease. In order for a stay to qualify as "short term" in most states, the guest must be staying for a period of thirty days or fewer. The function of an STR is to replace a stay in a hotel. Short-term rental properties are fully furnished and outfitted with everything a guest might need to "live" in the property for a few days or a week.

Most guests who stay in STRs are traveling, whether for business or pleasure. STRs used to exist mainly in vacation destinations, but they can now be found in almost any city across the world and are becoming nearly as commonplace as hotels. These properties differ from bed-and-breakfasts in that the owner of the STR property, commonly called the host, generally provides only the space. They do not provide meals, daily cleaning, or linen changing throughout the stay.

WHY WOULD A REAL ESTATE INVESTOR BUY AN STR?

The short answer is *cash flow*. Depending on the type and location, a property can generate upwards of three to five times more cash flow as an STR than as a traditional long-term rental (LTR). There are several key differences between short- and long-term rentals:

	SHORT-TERM RENTAL	LONG-TERM RENTAL
Occupant	Guest	Tenant
Furniture	Furnished	Usually unfurnished, although some may be furnished
	(It will have everything a guest needs to "live" in the property as if in their own home for a few days to a week, including sheets, towels, television, and cookware.)	
Utilities	Paid by the owner of the STR	Paid by the tenant
Housekeeping	A cleaning crew cleans the property and changes the linens after every stay	N/A
Success Driver	Reviews from previous guests	N/A

STR investing, if done correctly, can allow you to scale your portfolio exponentially more quickly than investing in LTRs alone. The heavy cash flow lets you accumulate down payments for your next investment faster without having to resort to private lending or long periods of saving.

This is the strategy that got me from zero to thirty doors—six STRs and twenty-four LTRs—five years ago and got me out of my corporate job in half that time. I started with no experience, no special training, no money from parents, and a marketing manager salary of $35,000. My husband and I were just regular folks. If we achieved financial independence, you can too.

In the following pages, you will learn how to invest in short-term rentals in order to turbocharge your cash flow and scale your portfolio in record time.

IS THIS THE RIGHT INVESTMENT FOR ME?

Before you spend any time researching markets and properties, make sure that real estate investing aligns with your life goals. I realized early on that I make a terrible corporate employee. Although I was raised to work my absolute hardest, I was not raised by employees; my dad and grandparents were self-employed. Since they hadn't failed without a W-2, I had no reason to think I would either. Stepping away from a steady salary didn't scare me. That is not the case for everyone. Many people are terrified to lose a corporate paycheck, and that's normal.

Whether you're self-employed or a W-2 employee, the scariest part of getting started in real estate investing is the decision to spend a big chunk, or perhaps all, of your savings on the down payment for your first property. That first property is scary. You're stepping into a new world, and you have no idea whether it will change your life for the better or take you down in complete and utter failure.

If you're married or in a long-term relationship, you'll need to make sure that your partner is on the same page with such a big leap. It will be very difficult for one partner to spend tens of thousands on down payments without the support of the other partner. In my relationship, neither of us had to convince the other that investing in real estate was worth exploring. We were in agreement on that from the very beginning. However, it did take us a few properties to understand which of us was best at playing which position in our investment business. Now that we've figured that out, we each have our specific role in the business, and we stick to it. My strength is identifying markets and properties at a high level. My husband's strength is the more granular analysis of the numbers on a property and management after the purchase. Identifying who should do what will be difficult at first. Analysis paralysis is a huge hurdle. The best advice I can give you is to not get bogged down in the minutiae and planning of every single step. You can spend your whole life analyzing and never do anything.

SEVEN STEPS TO FINANCIAL INDEPENDENCE USING STRS

Now that you've decided STRs are right for you, you may be wondering where to start. It can feel overwhelming when you think about everything self-managing an STR, potentially from out of state, entails. That's why I've broken it down into seven easy steps in this book:

1. Choosing your market
2. Choosing your property
3. Setting up your listings
4. Setting up your systems
5. Launching
6. Rolling with the punches
7. Scaling

By the end of this book, you'll be ready to invest in your first STR.

Chapter 2

CHOOSING THE RIGHT MARKET FOR YOU

Perfectionism kills every dream—better to just start.

—MIKE MICHALOWICZ, IN "PROFIT FIRST"

Short-term rentals, or vacation rentals, are a relatively new strategy when it comes to real estate investing. Although vacation rentals have been around for decades, it wasn't until the inception of Vrbo and Airbnb that traditional real estate investors began to invest more widely in them. If you're reading this book, chances are you want to explore the ins and outs of this strategy, but you aren't sure where to start.

The first thing you'll need to do is choose the type of market in which you want to invest. You'll begin by researching and analyzing factors like the average occupancy rate, price per night, and cost of properties in the area you're evaluating to determine whether an investment makes sense.

You've probably heard an anecdote or two from a friend who bought a house in the downtown area of their city and "is making a killing" on renting to conference-goers, traveling sports fans, and business travelers. "We're getting $500 a night," they might say. However, when probed, they cannot answer questions about things like occupancy rate, gross annual income, and expenses. A rate of $500 per night sounds great, but how many nights a year is the property booked? What is the monthly mortgage payment? How much do electricity and internet cost? Are there HOA fees? Does the $500 a night cover all expenses?

A random strategy yields random results. As a serious investor, you must do the proper research to choose the best market in which to invest based on data and historical information. Don't just buy a place close to Wrigley Field that will "pay for itself" because you're a giant Cubs fan.

THREE TYPES OF STR MARKETS

There are three core types of STR markets: metro markets, national fly-to vacation markets, and regional drive-to vacation and leisure markets. There is no right or wrong type of market for investing in STRs. However, all markets come with varying degrees of stability or volatility, based on a number of attributes. Each type has its pros and cons, which I will detail in this chapter.

Your choice of market will depend on what your goals are and how comfortable you are with risk. For example, I prefer the income and regulatory stability of the regional, drivable vacation rental market, although I know plenty of people who earn great returns from investing in metro markets, which are much riskier and have trickier STR regulations. Whichever type of market you choose, make sure you do the research before diving in.

Metro Markets

Metro markets are major metropolitan areas that attract many visitors but are not financially dependent on tourism. They have jobs and industries that support their local economies, and they usually have large and dense permanent-resident populations. Examples include New York, Los Angeles, Austin, and Nashville.

In metro markets, short-term rentals are a relatively new choice for renters who historically would have stayed in a hotel. These types of renters include professionals on business trips, traveling medical professionals, and locals taking "staycations." A significant pro of metro markets is this diverse pool of guests, as it offers a broad spectrum from which to obtain renters.

The inception of Vrbo and Airbnb presented quite the opportunity for early adopters of STRs in major metro markets, like my friend in Brooklyn. Their product was new and provided more space and comfort than standard hotel accommodations. Plus, at the time, such accommodations were scarce in their markets.

While metro markets have extremely high rewards in terms of cash flow, they are arguably the riskiest type of STR market, based on several factors. The historical preference for hotel rooms over privately owned homes, coupled with a dense permanent-resident population, has proven troublesome for many metro markets over the past decade. Additionally, metro markets have a far more volatile STR regulation structure than other types of markets. I know many metro-market STR investors who were shut down after a few short years of operation.

There are three main economic drivers of anti-STR regulations in major metropolitan areas:

1. **Hotel lobbyists:** Lobbying funded by major hotel chains is the largest source of anti-STR regulations in metro markets across the country. As hundreds of STRs have flooded the hospitality market and gained significant market share, hotels have made no small effort to eradicate them. By having lobbyists work to get bills introduced at the local level, the hotel chains have successfully curtailed the growth of the industry. This has resulted in cities' limiting the zones in which STRs are allowed, revoking permits, and, in some cases, banning them altogether.

2. **Disgruntled neighbors:** As STR investing has become more popular in many cities, properties on previously quiet residential streets have been converted into "mini hotels" and "party houses." Their permanent-resident neighbors have taken to city councils to voice their contempt for the perceived negative effects that STR investors have had on their neighborhoods. Negative local media coverage of these grievances and the few incidents that have caused them have created an adversarial relationship between STR owners and non-investor permanent residents.

3. **Lack of affordable housing due to Airbnb investors:** As long-term rental or primary-home properties have been acquired, renovated, and converted into STRs, property values in many metro markets have skyrocketed. Since it can be difficult to acquire these properties in major cities, they are often sold at a premium, and those premium-priced sales have caused rapid appreciation in the surrounding areas. While this sounds like a positive to investors, it has caused a severe affordable-housing issue for permanent residents in some markets, once again sending advocacy groups and locals to city councils with their complaints.

Another key consideration when investing in metro-market STRs is market saturation. In the rare metro market where STRs are largely unregulated, this is a very real possibility. When a market has gone from very few of these rentals to many over the course of a few years, and additional properties are being converted into STRs almost daily, market saturation is on the horizon. Of course, you always have the option of converting the property into a long- or medium-term rental if needed.

National Vacation Markets

National vacation markets are tourism-dependent. Think big, popular vacation markets that most travelers access by plane, such as Honolulu, Hawaii; Aspen, Colorado; and Orlando, Florida.

These markets are stable in terms of rental regulations because STRs have been part of the economic fabric for decades. Still, affluent permanent residents and large resort chains have pushed for STRs to be allowed only in certain areas. For example, Hawaii and Jackson Hole, Wyoming have strict regulations to keep their permanent residents happy. In fact, there are fewer than ten neighborhoods in Jackson Hole where short-term renting is allowed. This makes it difficult to find properties that are properly zoned to allow short-term renting and self-management of STRs.

While national vacation rental markets are quite lucrative during economic booms, they are the first to see a downward trend in a recession. As travelers tighten their purse strings, lavish fly-to vacations are traded for more affordable, closer-to-home destinations.

Regional Vacation Markets

In regional vacations markets, the majority of tourists arrive by car.

Examples include Gatlinburg, Tennessee; Panama City Beach, Florida; Big Bear Lake, California; and Branson, Missouri.

Regional leisure destinations are 100 percent financially dependent on tourism and have been for decades, just like the national vacation markets mentioned previously. There is little or no industry outside of tourism in these areas. However, one major difference from the national markets is that regional markets are much more affordable and more easily accessible.

Since these markets are often smaller towns, real estate prices tend to be cheaper than those found in national vacation rental markets. Additionally, many of these markets boast fewer permanent residents and more vacation renters, many of whom have been renting privately owned cabins, condos, and single-family homes rather than hotels since well before the inception of sites like Airbnb.

STR regulations are very accommodating in these markets, since local governments determined how to monetize STR income decades ago. City council clashes are therefore nonexistent. As a matter of fact, the small occupancy tax collected by these governments is so lucrative that it would be far too fiscally detrimental for them to regulate STRs.

On the surface, it would seem that metro markets are the best for STRs given their diverse pool of travelers. However, because of regulation issues in most metro areas, it's actually the regional, drivable vacation rental market that is the most stable investment. Regional markets are the most recession-resistant due to affordability and accessibility, which we will address in later pages.

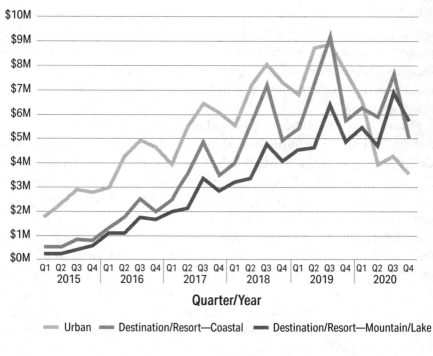

United States—Nights Booked (2015–2020)

Legend:
Urban — Destination/Resort—Coastal — Destination/Resort—Mountain/Lake

Source: Airdna.co

TOURISM AND RECESSION RESISTANCE

STRs are dependent on the tourism and travel industry, so it is important to ensure that there will be enough travelers for an STR to be profitable, even during economic downturns. Several factors contribute to market resilience.

First, we will take a look at the drivers of the past two economic downturns: the housing/financial crisis of 2008 and the COVID-19 pandemic of 2020–2021. During both of these economic downturns, the regional vacation market performed better than the metro and national vacation markets. That was thanks to its two pillars of recession resistance: affordability and accessibility.

1. **Affordability:** In the Great Recession of 2008, the disposable income of the average American family dropped dramatically. Many potential STR investors mistakenly assume that everyone stops going

on vacation when they have less disposable income. This is simply not the case. Travelers may no longer take a trip to Aspen, Disney World, or Hawaii, but they will still go on vacation—albeit to a more affordable vacation destination that does not require flights or expensive ski lift and theme park tickets. In other words, families go on local weekend getaways in a recession.

2. **Accessibility:** At the beginning of the COVID-19 pandemic in 2020, all STR markets took a forceful hit, but as reopenings started across the country, regional leisure markets outperformed both metro and national vacation markets. This time, while affordability was most definitely a factor, accessibility was the main driver of success.

After months of lockdowns, the entire population was bursting at the seams to get out of their homes. However, most Americans were not comfortable traveling to big metro areas with large concentrations of people, and they were even less comfortable with boarding flights and being confined with strangers for even a short period of time. Due to the fear of contracting the virus, travelers drove to their nearest vacation destination, in the comfort of their own vehicles, to rent single-family residences where they could be outside and enjoy themselves at a safe distance from other people.

DISCOVERING A MARKET'S INCOME POTENTIAL

When you have found an STR market that interests you, the first thing you need to do is examine the STR regulations in that market. You would be surprised at how many investors do not look into this before shopping for a property.

There are three levels of market strictness when it comes to STR permits: stringent, medium, and relaxed.

Stringent Markets

Stringent markets are those in which a battle is constantly being waged between STR owners and the city council. It's difficult to obtain a permit in these markets because of arduous, ever-changing processes and rules. Investors must monitor city council meetings closely, as anti-STR bills are passed often.

An example of a stringent market is Nashville. Clients call me on a weekly basis saying, "I am prequalified for up to $1 million. I found this $950,000 property that I'm in love with. Let's make an offer." More often than not, I have to dash their rhinestone-studded, guitar-pickin' dreams by breaking the news to them that their honky-tonk investment is not zoned for STRs. Even if a property *is* currently zoned for STRs, that doesn't mean it will be in the future.

Nashville is a city that experiences brutal clashes between city council members and STR owners. Each quarter, a new bill is introduced to the city council to shrink the geographic area where STRs are allowed, to limit the number of permits, or to cull the number of existing STRs altogether.

I had a situation recently where a developer began a project that consisted of fourteen purpose-built STR townhome units in the correct zoning. This property was in an ideal location: walkable to dining, shopping, and nightlife. Several of my clients purchased units in the pre-construction phase after having completed all necessary due diligence on zoning and income, and the papers were signed. Completion was scheduled for the following year. Six months into the contract, the city council passed a bill changing the zoning of this property to prohibit short-term rentals. The move would cause investors in this development, as well as several other developments across the city, to no longer be able to use the property as they had intended. None of the developers were allowing investors to withdraw their contracts without lawsuits either. It was a giant mess. Eventually, an agreement was reached that allowed the grandfathering of permits to be extended to developments that had broken ground within the past year, but the amount of stress and mental anguish these investors went through was not worth the investment.

The lesson here is that while stringent markets can be extremely lucrative, their ever-changing regulations need to be monitored constantly, which can be a full-time job in and of itself. The entire idea behind real estate investing is to generate passive income, so investors really have to weigh whether the income potential is worth the headache of keeping up with regulations in this type of market.

Moderate Markets

Moderate markets feature regulations that are stable and manageable for both STR owners and primary residents. These markets are very friendly toward STRs, as long as they are operated only where allowed by local zoning laws and with the correct permits.

Destin, Florida, where I own a property, is an example of a moderate market. There are clear boundaries designating where you can and cannot operate STRs. The main rule is that the city does not allow any STRs to be operated north of Highway 98, in order to preserve affordable and quiet housing for the few people who actually live in that market full-time. The beach and most main tourist attractions are south of Highway 98, so having an STR north of the highway wouldn't be ideal anyway.

To operate an STR in this market, I had to get a business license with the Florida Department of Revenue and an STR license with the city of Destin. An inspector had to approve the driveway for the number of parking spaces I can advertise, and a sign outside my property must state certain contact information. If I get too many tickets for violations like not pulling my trash cans in or having too many cars in the driveway, I can have my vacation rental license revoked.

Properties in moderate markets are great long-term investments as long as you don't skirt any rules on the front end and you pay your STR occupancy taxes, which we will discuss in a later chapter.

Relaxed Markets

Let me start this section by screaming from the rooftops that "relaxed" does not mean "free-for-all." Relaxed markets still have rules and regulations, but they are minimal, and revocation of STR licenses is typically unheard-of.

A great example of a relaxed market is the Great Smoky Mountains of East Tennessee. There are just two small geographical zonings within the cities of Pigeon Forge and Gatlinburg that do not allow STRs in order to preserve some housing for the locals.

Permits are usually required, but it shouldn't take more than a quick phone call to the county office to obtain one. These markets typically have as many (or more) STRs as they do permanent residences. The cities and counties are so dependent upon the local occupancy tax income from STRs that it's in their best interests to keep the regulations relaxed to make things easy for investors.

MARKET MATURITY

The second item to evaluate when choosing a market is its maturity. How long have STRs been the norm for travelers rather than hotels? How long have STRs been around? The earlier that STRs began to prosper in the market, the more mature the market is. The less mature a market is, the greater the chance of unfavorable STR regulations. The reason is simple: Less mature markets haven't had as much time to figure out an equilibrium between STR owners and permanent residents. Most metro markets fall into the less mature category, while true vacation rental markets will generally be the most mature. This translates to more favorable STR regulations and higher income potential.

FINDING TOURISM DATA

Since STR income is directly dependent upon the amount of tourism an area receives, tourism numbers are very important to your market analysis. To locate annual tourism numbers, visit your potential market's department of tourism website. If there is no data listed on the website, you can often call the department and ask someone to email you some tourism brochures and information. Gather data from as far back in time as possible. You want to have a clear picture of year-over-year tourism trends in the market.

Any of the major conference centers and tourist attractions in your potential market should also have visitor data. One of my markets, for example, is driven by tourism to Great Smoky Mountains National Park. The National Park Service has thorough visitation data on every park dating back to each one's opening. This will allow you to see how tourism in any National Park has been affected during every economic downturn in its history. Other great data sources are hotels, major theme parks, major-league sports teams, and universities.

FINDING POTENTIAL INCOME DATA

Several companies specialize in STR-specific data, including Mashvisor, Key Data, and AirDNA. The latter is the largest and most recognizable, and a resource I use often when analyzing STR market data. Of course, it's important to keep in mind that no data set is perfect. Try to stay away from property-specific analyzers at this point, and stick to data that show trends in your potential market as a whole. Getting caught up in the projections for one specific property at this stage is counterproductive, since you run the risk of analyzing an outlier and making a mistake based on atypical circumstances.

Another great way to obtain market data is through major national property managers, such as Vacasa, Evolve, and TurnKey. These are large start-ups, often backed by venture capitalists, with access to their own proprietary data. Call each of them and ask about the markets you are thinking of investing in. They will be able to provide you with even more market-wide data points.

The key here is to get as many good data points as possible. Any data you can get from sources that utilize the major online booking platforms will aid you in your analysis. Try to steer clear of rental projections from management companies that do not utilize the major booking platforms. Third-party data from companies that measure the performance of all STRs across multiple platforms, coupled with the Enemy Method (which we'll cover in Chapter Five), will give you a great income baseline for getting started with your property analysis.

Chapter 3

AGENTS, FINANCING, THE STR CONTRACT PROCESS

Great vision without great people is irrelevant.

—JIM COLLINS, "GOOD TO GREAT"

Now that you've narrowed down your markets, it's time to find an agent. While locating off-market deals on your own can be a great strategy, you'll need a market expert on your team for at least your first few purchases. An agent will help you identify specific properties and navigate the contract process, as well as familiarize you with the nuances of both STRs and your chosen market.

I once worked with a buyer who was an agent in another state. We analyzed quite a few deals and even got under contract on one or two, but we didn't end up closing due to the inspection. This client was initially very excited to purchase his first STR, so I was surprised when communication stopped for about a month and a half. He then called me out of the blue one day to tell me he had decided to get his license in my state and would be handling his own transactions. Slightly annoyed that he had wasted quite a bit of my time, I wished him well and promptly forgot about it.

A few months later, I came across his name while checking out some comps on one of the major booking platforms. I clicked on his listing and saw that he had bought a property in a development I was very familiar with—one that was infamous among agents in my market for its problems.

The neighborhood was in a great location, and all the properties were of good quality and workmanship, but the development wasn't close to any major attractions. This neighborhood was known for the severe and ongoing water issues that the HOA had been "addressing" and "working to rectify" for years, problems that were not easily fixable. The area was on a community water system, which consists of a series of wells that fill one or two on-site water towers that supply water to all the properties. The developer had overbuilt the community for the capacity of the water system. Because of this, when the properties were filled with renters during the peak summer and holiday seasons, they would run out of water without warning. In order for the cabins to regain water access, every single property would have to refrain from turning on faucets and flushing toilets until the water towers had fully refilled, which could take anywhere from a few hours to an entire day.

If this buyer had a local expert in his corner during the purchase, he would have known about the water issue. I never would have let him make an offer on that property had I been asked. The few bucks he made in commission on that transaction were likely outweighed by the refunds he had to issue to guests for not having water on their vacation.

In another instance, a former client of mine decided to go directly to the listing agent on a new-construction property he saw on the Multiple Listing Service (MLS). Had he mentioned it to me, I could have told him that two of my previous clients had major issues with the builder on that project. These issues included lawsuits with previous developers, building over lot lines, not obtaining the proper permits to build, not honoring the state-required one-year builder warranty, and—the icing on the cake—installing a dehumidifier in the pool room that was not robust enough for the job. This resulted in so much condensation that the electrical shorted out, the brand-new HVAC died, and guests' children threw up repeatedly due to the lack of air circulation, which in turn resulted in calls to poison control.

The key takeaway from these anecdotes is that you must have a market expert on your team to provide the ancillary information a spreadsheet can't analyze for you. Trying to save a few bucks on buyer-agent commission can cost you dearly in missed information that can significantly impact your investment, and the consequences may or may not be fixable once you own the property.

FINDING AN AGENT

Your agent should be experienced, well versed in STRs, and familiar with investor clients and STR analysis. So how do you find expert investor-oriented agents? The answer is simple: Ask other investors. At some point during your analysis to determine where to invest and how, you're going to come across an investor who has successfully done what you're trying to do. Ask them who their agent is. Here are a few other great resources for finding expert investor-oriented agents right from your couch:

1. **The BiggerPockets forums:** If you've bought this book, there's a good chance you are familiar with BiggerPockets and its excellent educational resources for investors, including its online forums, where investors share information on virtually every aspect of real estate investing. Search for the market you're interested in, and you'll find at least a handful of successful investors in that market discussing their experiences. Ask them who their agent is and, while you're at it, for any other information and experiences they are willing to share on investing in that area. However, take all information you receive with a grain of salt. For example, if your target market is Big Bear Lake and you strike up a conversation with a professional STR property manager in that area, they're most likely going to tell you it's impossible to self-manage an STR, throw out a few horror stories, and scare you to death. A good rule of thumb for choosing investors to reach out to is to look at their post count. How many posts do they have? The more posts they have, the more engaged they are with the investor community. More important than the number of posts, though, is the number of upvotes they have. If the number of upvotes far outweighs the number of posts, that means they contribute the most valuable content. A user who has 600 posts

and 1,000 upvotes is probably a better source than one who has 300 posts and 25 upvotes.

2. **STR owner Facebook groups:** Users in these groups fall into one of two categories: (1) legitimate investors who are utilizing their STRs as cash-flow vehicles, or (2) vacation homeowners who treat their properties as their pride and joy, meet each guest personally, and would never create a listing for their rentals on Airbnb. You'll find plenty of valuable information in these groups (especially when it comes to vendor recommendations) if you're willing to sort through which posters are legitimate and which are not. BiggerPockets also has a number of Facebook groups for their various communities— join the Real Estate Rookies Facebook group if you're new to the STR world!

3. **STR webinars and masterminds:** There are plenty of webinars and virtual mastermind groups where new investors can learn the ropes from more seasoned investors. Find one that is relevant to the market you are interested in and start asking successful investors for recommendations. The best place to get great information is from investors who are already successful with the type of investment you're interested in acquiring—and remember, you won't need to pay exorbitant fees for this education.

4. **The booking platforms themselves:** When my husband and I first started, there was precious little information on buying and self-managing STRs as a long-term wealth-building strategy. Forum posts and Facebook groups were limited, so we logged on to the major rental platforms and messaged every owner in our target investment area. Our messages were mostly greeted with silence or annoyance, but two or three owners did respond positively. One even took the time to get on the phone with us and explain how she self-managed her properties from six hours away. This owner was in her 60s and not particularly technologically savvy. Still, she managed her three STRS remotely while holding down a full-time healthcare job and caring for a disabled spouse. Her one act of kindness was the catalyst for us to pull the trigger on our first STR investment. So while most people will ignore you or tell you to buzz off, keep reaching out. It takes only one or two responses to get a lot of valuable information.

Once you have a few agent names, it's time to make some calls to see which one is going to be the best fit for your STR investment journey. Below are the most important questions to ask when interviewing an agent, as well as a few pitfalls to avoid.

Questions

1. **How many properties do you sell a year?** Good agents have a lot of clients, so you want a busy agent, not one who can spend all day on the phone with you. The more deals they close, the more relationships they have—not only with other investors but also with the other agents in their market (which means access to off-market deals). You've heard of the 80/20 rule: 20 percent of people do 80 percent of the work. With real estate agents, it's more like the 98/2 rule: 2 percent of agents are doing 98 percent of the business. This is beneficial to buyer clients, especially in a hot market, because in multiple-offer situations, a listing agent is more likely to award the contract to the buyer's agent they are most comfortable working with. The agent no one knows has the hardest time winning contracts. In addition, the number of deals an agent closes in a year speaks to how good they are at their job.

2. **What percentage of your closings are for investors?** Investors are an entirely different beast than primary-home buyers. If an agent closes fifty deals a year but forty-five of them are primary homes, they might not be the best choice for you. Ideally, you should seek out an agent who works exclusively with investors. Several years ago, I was coming off a year of selling $50 million in STR investments. I took on a primary-home buyer as a favor to a friend, and the buyer fired me because I didn't know where to find the serial number on a $50,000 mobile home. While it bothered me at the time, they were right to fire me. I had sold $50 million in STR investments, not $50 million in mobile homes. They needed an expert mobile home agent, which I was not. I don't take that type of client anymore because that's not what I specialize in. Ideally, the agent in the market you choose will have that same awareness.

3. **Are you an investor yourself? Do you self-manage your units?** While a no to either question is not a deal breaker by any means, an agent who is also an investor will understand the process that buyers go through when purchasing an STR. If they are an investor agent,

ask whether they self-manage. Again, if they don't that's certainly not a deal breaker, but if they do self-manage, their experience will be invaluable to you throughout the transaction and well after closing. Be wary of agents who are property managers or whose brokers are property managers, as they may try to sign you up for their management program. Unless you are going through a full-service turnkey provider, the right agent should not stand to benefit from how you choose to manage your property after closing.

Common Mistakes

Good agents are selective when choosing their clients. To ensure that you present yourself as an ideal client, avoid the following missteps:

1. **Immediately asking for a discount or commission rebate toward closing costs.** Recently, one of my favorite past clients referred me to a friend. After chatting about the market for a few minutes, the friend asked, "Will you give me cash back towards closing out of your commission?" I told him no. My team and I do much more than just write contracts and show houses. I spend a lot of time analyzing properties and training clients on how to self-manage. Many moving parts and a ton of client communication go into those two tasks alone. It's not that I won't do discounts, but I won't do them for someone I just met. I'm happy to do them for clients I have a great relationship with or if I need to throw in a few bucks to get my buyer through a stalemate with the listing side. I want my clients to get great properties and to be successful. That being said, someone who leads by asking for a discount is someone who does not value my time and services and will probably be difficult to satisfy throughout the transaction, no matter how much time and effort I put in. Discount agents do discount work—it's as simple as that.

   While we're on the topic, if you are a licensed agent in another state, asking to apply a referral fee to your deal is not always appropriate. Although it's not wrong per se, doing this can keep you from gaining access to the best deals. For example, I personally invest in a market I do not live in, in a state where I am a licensed agent. Instead of doing all of my own deals and collecting full buyer agent commission, I use an amazing agent in that market. In more than twenty transactions, I have never asked this agent to pay me a referral fee, and I never will. Why? Because I don't get in his pocket, I often receive the first phone call when a good deal pops up on or off the market. Having access to deals is more important to me than getting a few bucks off his commission.

2. **Demanding off-market deals.** We are in a hot real estate market at the moment. Every single one of my five markets, across five states, sees multiple offers on appropriately priced properties within a day of hitting the market. In this economy, off-market STR properties are like the Holy Grail. Sellers know that a good STR property is worth a premium, and they have very little incentive not to list it to get multiple bids. When I get off-market listings, I first reward my repeat clients with them, and then I reward the clients who are nicest to me. That second part sounds a little silly, but I'd much rather send deals to nice people than to mean ones. When a brand-new buyer schedules a consultation with me and demands access to my off-market deals with very little else to say, I politely get off the phone. Also, when it comes to STRs, just because a deal is off-market does not mean it's a better deal; it simply means there will be fewer competitive buyers with access to it. Only the buyers who are the most serious about purchasing (usually the most experienced buyers) will get access to those deals.

3. **Working with multiple agents.** One rock-star agent is more valuable to you as a buyer than twenty mediocre agents. I've been burned several times by clients asking me to send them my top five picks for cash flow on the market. I spend time analyzing and compiling the list, only to find out that they made an offer on a property I deemed a poor investment and purposely skipped because another agent's auto-update platform blasted it to them. "That agent sent us this property, so we chose to offer with them, but we will use you for the next one" is the typical justification. If that client does come back around, I usually refuse to take them on. A good agent's time is worth a lot. If you prove to be a waste of it, you will likely lose that relationship before it even starts.

FINANCING

Now that you've hired the best agent for the job, it's time to get your financing in order. The number one thing to remember is that you cannot make an offer on a property without securing a preapproval from the lender.

Many buyers try to get away with writing offers without obtaining pre-approval first. "We can figure out the financing later," they say. That may work for distressed properties in Omaha, Nebraska, but in a tight STR market, there is usually no time to waste. If you want your offer to be considered, you must include a preapproval letter or proof of funds. No seller wants to tie up their property for even a few days with a buyer who can't close. Don't get under contract if you aren't sure your financing is sound.

All the traditional methods of acquiring financing (cash, conventional loans, commercial loans, private lenders, hard-money lenders) are available for STR investments. In addition, there is one loan product that is unique to STR opportunities if you meet certain requirements, the most important being that you stay in the property for a specified number of days per year. This product is the 10 percent down vacation home loan. That's right: 10 percent down.

It's a conventional Fannie Mae/Freddie Mac–backed product, but be sure to check with a licensed lender on all of these stipulations to ensure that you are following Fannie/Freddie rules. Generally speaking, you qualify for a 10 percent down vacation home loan if the property meets the following requirements:

1. It must be more than sixty-five miles from your primary home.
2. You must occupy the property for some portion of the year. (The number of days is not specified in current guidelines, but ask your lender for the most up-to-date details.)
3. The property must be a one-unit dwelling, so no duplexes, triplexes, or fourplexes.
4. The property must be suitable for year-round occupancy.
5. You must have exclusive control of the property (meaning you can't sign control over to someone else with a lease).
6. The property cannot be placed with a property management company.
7. You may utilize only one vacation home loan per market (meaning you can take out multiple vacation home loans as long as each property is in a different market).

Under current Fannie Mae guidelines, there is nothing prohibiting owners from renting out their property on the major booking platforms during the times when they are not occupying it. With that being said, Fannie Mae and Freddie Mac do limit the number of vacation home loans that each lender can execute. Just make sure you are clear and transparent with your lender about your intentions with the property to ensure that you are following the guidelines properly. And before you even ask: Yes, you have to pay private mortgage insurance (PMI) on anything with a down payment of less than 20 percent. However, you could pay it all up front for a fairly modest fee at closing, or you could get the PMI removed by obtaining a broker price opinion (BPO) in a year or two. A BPO should not be confused with an appraisal—a BPO is an opinion on the value of the property generated by a qualified professional, such as a real estate broker or representative of the mortgage company. BPOs are less rigorous and less tightly regulated than appraisals. If the BPO shows that the property has appreciated 10 percent and you now have 20 percent equity in the property, most lenders will knock off the PMI.

One type of loan that isn't commonly used in LTR investing but is often used in STR investing is the jumbo loan, which exceeds the limits set by the Federal Housing Finance Agency (FHFA). Designed and most commonly used to finance large and/or luxury properties, jumbo loans differ from conventional loans in that they are not guaranteed by or eligible to be sold to Fannie Mae or Freddie Mac. Additionally, the interest rates on jumbo loans are a little bit higher, and the buyer has to meet more rigorous qualifications compared to those for a conventional loan. The jumbo loan limit is different in every state, depending on real estate values. For example, the jumbo loan limit is much higher in New York than it is in Alabama.

Financing Strategies

- **Partnerships:** Partnerships can be a great way to get into a property with little money down. In order to partner on a property with both parties on the contract, you'll need to obtain conventional or commercial financing, as second home/vacation home financing is available only to partners who can prove that they are related. There are a number of ways that partnerships can be structured on STR purchases, the most common being the money partner plus sweat-equity partner method. The term is self-explanatory, but I'll go into a bit more detail: The money partner obtains the loan and the contract on the property, while the sweat-equity partner performs the day-to-day management functions. The process after closing looks something like this: The money partner will hold what I call a "mini-mortgage" with the sweat-equity partner in the amount of the sweat-equity partner's half of the down payment. The sweat-equity partner will pay the mini-mortgage to the money partner until their half of the down payment is paid off. At that point, the rental income profits will revert to being split in true 50/50 fashion after expenses. Profits can be paid out to each partner monthly, quarterly, or yearly, depending on what has been agreed upon by the partnership. Remember, it is always a good idea to have documents outlining the terms of the partnership drafted by an attorney licensed in your state. Some partners are satisfied with a handshake deal, but even the best of partnerships can go sour, and it's always best practice to have everything in writing.

- **BRRRR:** For those unfamiliar with the term, BRRRR stands for "buy, rehab, rent, refinance, repeat." This strategy involves paying cash for a property in need of significant repairs, making those repairs and forcing a large amount of appreciation, renting the property, refinancing the property for its new after-repair value (ARV), and pulling all your cash out to do it again. Essentially, you're getting the property for free, because after the refinance, you are pulling out the same amount of cash (or more) that you put into the property and rehab. (For a deeper dive into the topic, check out David Greene's book *Buy, Rehab, Rent, Refinance, Repeat: The BRRRR Rental Property Investment Strategy Made Simple*.)

Whether you can use this strategy to invest in an STR depends on conditions in your chosen market. Generally speaking, you will need a very high budget to pay cash for a property that will make a good STR, even after rehab. In some markets it will be impossible due solely to the price of real estate, even for properties that need a lot of rehab. However, I suppose if you have enough money, BRRRR is an option in any market. Just make sure that if you are buying to BRRRR, you understand the amount of work and coordination it will take to succeed with this strategy. I've had many clients who wanted to BRRRR yet balked at the cost of rehab. Don't be flippant about the BRRRR method. While it can yield amazing results and be a great way to scale, it takes a lot of hard work to pull off.

Metro markets typically lend themselves to the BRRRR method better than vacation markets. That's because in order for a property to be a viable BRRRR candidate, you'll need to acquire it for significantly less than market value. How does that happen? When the property is "distressed"—in other words, the owner is facing financial hardship and needs to unload the property quickly—the seller might be willing to accept less than market value.

Although I do have clients who have successfully completed several BRRRRs (and I've done a few myself), there are simply fewer opportunities to execute this method in vacation markets than in metro markets. In vacation markets, the majority of properties will either be second homes or existing investment properties. Therefore, if an owner gets into financial trouble, these properties will be the first ones they sell, for close to market value. Only after all other avenues have been exhausted will the primary-home property become "distressed" and a candidate for a below-market-value acquisition. While it is possible for second homes and investment properties to become distressed, it just does not happen nearly as often as with primary homes.

BUYING SIGHT UNSEEN

In some markets, you'll have plenty of time to shop, walk properties, and analyze them before making an offer, but in more popular markets, it won't be possible for you to see every property that interests you before it goes under contract. If you want to acquire a property in a tight seller's market, you'll need to get comfortable with the idea of making an offer sight unseen. This means that you put in an offer without viewing the property in person.

Some investors are comfortable with this, and some aren't. If you are new to STR investing and interested in a hot market, make an exploratory trip to spend a few days in the area. Drive around, visit some of the most popular tourist attractions and restaurants, and learn which locations you prefer. Familiarize yourself with the market so that as properties come up for sale, you're prepared to make an offer.

When a property does hit the market, ask your agent to take a video for you. Request that they shoot a 360-degree view from the front yard so you can see the surrounding properties, and a 360-degree view of the rooms to get a better idea of how big they are and how the space flows. Additionally, have them take a photo of the serial number on the HVAC unit, which will tell you how old it is before you make an offer. From the videos, try to identify anything that may be worn out or broken. Remember, if you do make an offer and get under contract, a licensed professional will conduct a detailed home inspection. Real estate agents are not licensed home inspectors or contractors, so they cannot be expected to catch every item that may need attention in a preliminary video.

In some markets, most of the properties will be existing STRs. If this is the case, then no one—be they a Realtor, a home inspector, or a buyer—is allowed to enter the property if it is rented. In hot markets, a property could go on sale on a Friday, have a guest in the house until the following Wednesday, and go under contract before any buyers or agents are able to view or shoot video of the property.

If this is the case for a property you're interested in, there are a few actions you can take. The first is to ask for a viewing contingency. This means that the seller will allow you a certain amount of time after accepting your offer to view the property. If you don't like the property, you can terminate the contract with earnest money refunded. However, if there are multiple offers on a property, a viewing contingency can weaken your offer. When there are multiple offers and a viewing contingency would reduce your chances of winning the contract, ask for a fourteen-day inspection period. This will allow enough time for you and/or your agent to take a look at the property. If you opt to go this route, you will still need to have the home inspection performed, but in the worst-case scenario, you can terminate based on the inspection if you need to back out of the contract. This isn't an air-tight strategy, as the seller does have the ability to push back, but ultimately it wouldn't be in their best interest to tie up the property. In most cases, although they may be annoyed, you'll be able to exit the contract based on the inspection and get your earnest money back.

BUILD OR BUY EXISTING?

In today's hot real estate market, most existing properties receive multiple offers at or above asking price within a couple of days. This can be discouraging to new investors and can entice them to consider building a property instead. However, undertaking a custom build in a brand-new market is probably not the wisest investment move. What if you decide you don't like owning an STR in that market? What if you've built something that is pleasing to you but not ideal to potential buyers and/or renters? If it doesn't work out, you could always sell the property, but that's a lot of time and resources wasted to end up with no long-term income stream. My advice is to gain a little experience in your chosen market before you jump into the custom-build pool.

If you do decide to build, make sure you explore all avenues and costs associated with new constructions in that particular market. In beach markets, for example, there may be an additional cost associated with building the lot up a few feet to protect against flooding. In mountain markets, where lots are often steep, you can spend well into six figures just on grading and retaining walls. In metro markets, you have to be very careful about zoning and HOAs. Interview builders, engineers, and other investors who have built properties if you can. The last thing you want to do is buy a cheap lot, only to discover that you'll have to lay out thousands of dollars more just to ready it for building—at a great detriment to your ROI.

An alternative to a custom-build project is the spec home, that is, a home built by a builder or developer with the intent of selling it immediately. Sometimes spec homes are one-offs, while others are inside full neighborhoods that are reserved by the lot. Spec homes are a middle ground between an existing home and a custom build. You will get the new home aesthetic and usual builder's warranty without the wear and tear of an existing construction, but you won't have to go through the headache of sourcing plans and a builder in addition to all the decision making a custom build requires. Developments that are purpose-built for STR use are becoming more common in each of the STR market types. I'd recommend buying spec homes only in communities that are being developed specifically for STR properties rather than in traditional HOAs. Traditional HOAs, which have a higher number of primary residents, may be less receptive to STRs in the neighborhood, which could lead to a ban on STRs in the community a few years down the road.

Contracts on New Construction

One thing to be especially careful of when it comes to new construction is the nonstandard developer contract. Each state has a standard set of real estate contracts and forms for both existing and new construction through the National Association of Realtors (NAR). These standard forms are designed to protect both buyer and seller should either side act in bad faith during the contract period. But when a builder or developer is building a set of properties, they'll sometimes have their own attorney draw up the contracts. Beware of these nonstandard contracts. Oftentimes, they are one-sided and allow the builder many liberties and much leeway while locking the buyer into a contract without any real objection or negotiation power—even if the developer makes changes to the property that the buyer did not agree to in the original contract.

During the coronavirus shutdown, many businesses went under and investors' financial situations changed. Investors who had entered into a new-construction contract prior to the COVID-19 outbreak found themselves suddenly unable to qualify for the property for which they were under contract. Those who used the standard NAR forms were able to get out of their contract by invoking the financing contingency. Yet those who were bound by proprietary developer contracts didn't have the benefit of that standard financing contingency and lost tens of thousands of dollars in deposits.

Nonetheless, proprietary contracts are not inherently bad, and many result in an amazing finished product. It is just very important to have your attorney review any nonstandard purchase contracts. Relying on your agent to interpret a contract is not enough, as Realtors are not licensed attorneys. In some states, "practicing law without a license" is an offense that can warrant the revocation of an agent's license.

CONDOS

Many investors are scared off by the word "condo" because they immediately associate the term with exorbitant association fees. Before you write off condos completely, learn what is included in the fees. A two-bedroom condo with a $500-a-month HOA fee sounds like a bad deal at first blush, but sometimes condo fees include cable and internet or some of the utility costs, in addition to amenities. If cable and internet—which can run about $200 a month for a two-bedroom property—are included, the HOA fees start to make more sense. Condo fees may also include the insurance on the building and exterior items, so insurance premiums could be cheaper for the owner.

Condo financing can be difficult to obtain in some markets. In vacation markets, many condos are located in buildings called condotels. As the name suggests, condotels are typically condo buildings that are comprised mostly of rentals or investment properties. You can find buildings like these in vacation and tourism-driven markets. Although it's impossible to determine if a property is considered a condotel by Fannie Mae and Freddie Mac standards just by looking at it, many condotels have check-in desks and in-house vacation rental management companies. The only way to definitively determine whether a property is a condotel is to have the HOA manager fill out a "condo questionnaire" provided by your lender. Condotels are non-warrantable, meaning they do not meet the criteria for conventional lending terms. Many lenders find them too risky, which makes financing difficult. You'll often have to put down more than the standard 20 percent, and you'll need either a portfolio loan or a commercial loan.

To find out whether a condo is non-warrantable, your lender will have to request a "condo questionnaire" from the HOA. A property must meet the following criteria in order to be warrantable:

1. No single entity owns more than a certain percentage of the units. (The number can change from year to year when Fannie Mae releases new guidelines. It is currently 10 percent, but your lender will be able to give you the exact number at the time of your purchase.)
2. The project has fewer than four units.
3. The unit is a detached condo.
4. At least 50 percent of the units are either second homes or primary residences, not investment properties.
5. The HOA is not involved in any lawsuits.
6. No more than 25 percent of the owners in the project are delinquent on HOA dues.
7. Commercial space accounts for less than 35 percent of the square footage of the project.

In markets where there are many condotels, it is possible to find local lenders with great options for financing. Call around to local banks and mortgage companies, and you'll eventually find one that offers a warrantable condo product.

STRATEGIES

Real estate investing is great because there are many different ways to make money, but don't get caught up in trying to execute several strategies in a single purchase. I've had investors tell me they are looking for a

BRRRR buy-and-hold fix-and-flip mobile home park that they can house hack and use as an STR at the same time (ha!).

I know we are talking about STRs here, but I'd like to give an example using an LTR that I bought several years ago. In 2016, I was in the market for a property that needed rehab—something I could get for below market and fix up. While I was searching, a property hit the MLS at a decent price. It had been kept up by the previous owners and didn't need any work. There was no potential value-add; it was listed for market value. I checked the rent comps in the neighborhood and made an offer at asking price. Why? Because the price I was getting it for compared to the market rent made sense, so I locked it up. I didn't play around and try to get it for a significant discount so that I could force appreciation. Of all the doors I currently own, that property has the highest cash flow of any of my LTRs to date. The mortgage is $600 a month, and it rents for $1,650 a month. If I had wasted time trying to turn it into a value-add property when it made perfect sense, cash-flow wise, to buy it the way it was, I would not have acquired the property.

In another transaction, I bought a foreclosure that had been on the market for nearly a year and needed a significant amount of rehab. I successfully forced about $150,000 in appreciation using that approach. Two different deals presented two different opportunities using two distinctly different strategies.

It's okay to use different strategies based on each deal, but if you try to execute too many strategies at once, you'll never find the right fit. Real estate investors must be fluid and adaptable. I have seen many investors pass up great deals because the property needed a little rehab, or didn't need enough rehab, or the numbers were .0001 percent off on their spreadsheet. Don't pass up a great opportunity because you're too rigid in your approach.

It's also important to keep in mind that what works in one market does not always work in another. You might be able to successfully execute a BRRRR STR in Raleigh, North Carolina, to cash flow $1,000 a month, while you can buy a relatively turnkey furnished property in Joshua Tree, California, to cash flow $3,000 a month. Different markets require different strategies, and no one strategy is inherently better than any other. You have to adapt to each market. In some markets, you'll be able to negotiate price significantly; in others, you'll be competing with multiple offers on every property. Don't pass up an opportunity in a seller's market just because you can't get the owner to come down 15 percent on the asking price. What you need to focus on is still cash-on-cash return—how much you are putting in at the required price to acquire the property versus how much you are getting out. The difference between a successful and unsuccessful real estate investor is closing deals. And in order to close deals, you have to dig yourself out of analysis paralysis, adapt to your market, and start pulling some triggers.

NUANCES OF THE CONTRACT PROCESS

Now that you have analyzed and determined your market and strategy, it's time to start writing some contracts. For the most part, the contract process for purchasing an STR is the same for purchasing any other residential property, with a few minor differences. In this section we will go over the nuances that are specific to STR contracts.

The Inspection and Due Diligence Period

Since STRs are residential properties and not commercial (in most cases), the inspection/due diligence period will work as it would for almost any other residential property. You'll get home, pest, radon, septic, well, and any other necessary inspections that are typical in the market in which you are buying.

In some states, like Texas and California, there is a so-called option period during which a buyer can terminate a contract for any reason whatsoever within a certain time frame, with no recourse from the seller. This is not typical in most states, so it's important not to assume that you can back out of a deal on a whim. That's a great way to lose your earnest money. Ask your agent about the rules in the state where you're buying before going under contract. In states where there is no option period, only an inspection period, you cannot terminate the contract over something that is not a material defect of the home. I know one investor who lost $70,000 in deposits before any inspection was ever done on the home because "I found something I liked better in another market" was not a contingency of the contract. Why is this relevant to STR purchases? Because at the end of the inspection period, you cannot terminate the contract over items like "the furniture is worn out," or "the rental potential is unsatisfactory," or, my personal favorite, "after further evaluation, it has become apparent that this home is not suited to be an STR."

I recently had an investor client who went under contract on a beautiful new-construction property. He decided to back out because he had come to the conclusion that he didn't like the floor plan. Unfortunately, in the state where he was buying, that was not a good enough reason to get your earnest money back. I had to comb the inspection report for any believable defect that would allow him to fall out of the contract, which is difficult on a brand-new build that is still under warranty. It was challenging and took some convincing, but we were able to get his earnest money back in the end.

The moral of that story is, if you decide to terminate a contract on the basis of potential income, furniture, or other objections that do not pertain to the property's deficiencies, the path of least resistance (and the path to getting your earnest money back) is always to point to material defects found in the inspection report. If you start throwing out issues with floor plans, hypothetical situations, or nebulous concerns—like how well a property will perform as an STR—the seller will, at the very least, contest your earnest money refund. At worst, they can hold you for specific performance. Read: They'll sue you. I have never seen this happen, but it can.

Contracts on Furnished Properties

Many STRs, especially in vacation markets, may have previously been vacation homes or STRs and will therefore come fully furnished. Some inexperienced sellers and agents will try to assign value to the furniture in the real estate contract. For example, they'll suggest "Property price is $500,000 unfurnished, or $550,000 furnished." Furniture is personal property and, therefore, in the eyes of any lender, can have no value in a real estate contract. It can't even be mentioned in the real estate contract. Furniture must be addressed in a separate document that does not go to the lender. Additionally, furniture cannot be a negotiation point during the inspection period because—you guessed it—furniture is not real estate.

Assigning value to furniture is an issue seen mainly in metro markets where the trading of STRs is relatively new. In mature vacation markets, where trading STRs has been commonplace for decades, it's expected that the furniture comes with the property in as-is condition. The best way to address furniture is to have both buyer and seller sign a separate bill of sale stating that all contents of the property will come with the property in as-is condition at no additional charge, or at the cost of $1.

"Honoring" of Future Bookings After Closing

There are a few scenarios that come up very often in STR transactions regarding future bookings:

1. The seller wants the buyer to honor any existing bookings after closing.
2. The seller wants to "transfer" future bookings to the buyer but retain an X percent procurement fee for the bookings.
3. The seller wants the property to remain with the current property management company for a set amount of time after closing (usually thirty days, sometimes more).
4. The buyer wants to take over the seller's existing Airbnb and Vrbo accounts to retain their reviews.
5. The seller wants to continue managing the property for the buyer after closing.

Ideally none of the above requests will arise. While it can seem enticing to take on an existing book of business, there are a few things to consider. Let's take a closer look at the pros and cons of each scenario.

1. The seller wants the buyer to honor any existing bookings after closing. This is the least annoying of the scenarios. In this case, the buyer would create their Airbnb and Vrbo profiles before closing. The seller would then send a message to all future booked guests telling them that the property has been sold and sharing a link to the buyer's new listings for rebooking. Make sure to get all booking details including dates and pricing from the seller before agreeing to the arrangement. You want to ensure that the property has been booked at market prices and that the seller has not accepted any bookings for thirty days or longer. (Once a guest has inhabited a property for thirty days, they can retain tenants' rights, which will require a full eviction in the event that the guest refuses to leave.) It's also possible that the previous seller may not have screened guests as well as you intend to, and you could end up with unruly guests.

    While a fully booked calendar sounds nice, I recommend that you do not agree to this request. If you are buying in the right market, you will not need the seller's bookings. Plus, requiring guests to cancel and rebook with another owner is going to annoy them before they even check in. And if you, as the new owner, have made any changes to the property, it is possible that the guests will not be pleased, which will negatively affect your reviews. Don't leave this to chance by accepting future bookings—start fresh from the beginning.

On the flip side, many buyers will ask sellers to stop booking the property at the time that a contract to purchase is signed. This is also unreasonable. Why on earth would the seller stop booking the property when the property has yet to go through the inspection or appraisal process? What if the buyer terminates the contract because buyer and seller cannot come to an agreement on inspection items? What if the property does not appraise? What if the buyer decides to finance five Lambos before closing and can no longer qualify for the loan? If the seller stops taking bookings, they stand to lose a significant amount of money, and if there is any discrepancy in the contingencies, they are more likely to try to keep the buyer's earnest money. You as the buyer need to understand why a seller would not agree to stop taking bookings on the first day of the contract period. Not pushing them too hard on this front will save you a lot of headaches during the contract process if you decide that you need to terminate the contract.

2. In some cases, not only will the seller request to "transfer" bookings to the future buyer, but they will also request to keep a percentage of the income from those bookings as a finder's fee. Never agree to this. I have been through this scenario many times with clients. Sometimes buyers will think, "Hmm, they have $15,000 worth of bookings to give me, and they want to keep $5,000. That's not such a bad deal." This never ends well for the buyer. It leads to situations in which sellers bring checks to closing outside of the escrow, or buyers agree to send money to the sellers after closing. I have seen this end in lawsuits between buyer and seller because someone didn't stick to what was laid out in the contract.

In some cases, the seller will want to keep the initial deposits they received on the bookings before the sale. In my experience, this means that the seller has already spent those deposits. The absolute cleanest way to handle any transfer of bookings is for the buyer to create their new Airbnb and Vrbo listings and for the seller to send a cancellation email to all future guests that includes the new listing link for rebooking. This way, there is no money being exchanged outside of escrow between buyer and seller. All deposits are returned to the platform they were booked on, and fresh bookings can begin on the buyer's new listing, with neither buyer nor seller anxiously waiting to see if the other will hold up their end of the deal.

3. The seller wants the property to remain with the current property management company for a predetermined period of time after closing. We see this often in vacation markets that have many traditional property management companies. In most circumstances, it is not legal for the seller to require this. Check with a local real estate attorney to understand the relevant laws in your state.

    That said, it's not always worth the time and expense to go through a legal process over this matter. Usually the contract will require that the property stay with the management company for a set period of time to accommodate future booked dates. In this case, the buyer will receive whatever the usual owner/company split is (anywhere from 80/20 to 60/40 in some markets), plus any maintenance and fees incurred during that time. This scenario usually arises because the property management company has an agreement with the seller that states the seller will have to pay a large fee if they do not keep the property with said management company for a specific amount of time after closing. You as the investor have to decide whether the property is worth the trouble of dealing with the management company for a month or two after closing. If the property is in a hot market and has multiple offers, this might just be something you have to agree to in order to win the bid.

    Sometimes these requirements can be negotiated in exchange for a higher purchase price. Another strategy would be to have a longer close date so the seller can give the management company notice of the sale. That way, the clock starts ticking while the property is still under contract.

4. Newbie STR buyers will often ask to take over the seller's existing Airbnb and Vrbo accounts in order to retain their reviews. There is no way to truly transfer accounts between individuals anyway, but allow me to explain why you shouldn't try.

    ▪ These accounts are tied to bank accounts, Social Security numbers, and tax ID numbers. It is not a good idea to allow anyone access to these accounts, no matter how small the window of time before they're deleted or changed.

- Just because a listing has some good reviews does not mean that it has been properly managed. If the seller has historically been slow to respond to inquiries, has made too many cancellations, or has had any complaints against them, this will affect the algorithms that determine how high up on the list of available properties a listing appears when a traveler does a search. It is possible for a property to have good reviews but still fall low in the search results due to poor management behind the scenes. Good reviews won't get you anywhere if no one can see your listing because it's fifteen pages back in the search results.

5. The seller wants to continue managing the property for the buyer after closing. Just say no. I shouldn't have to explain why this is a terrible idea. Aside from the issue of not being in control of your own ROI, have you ever done a real estate transaction where you wanted to be wrapped up in a business agreement with the party on the other side of the table? I didn't think so. Rookie mistake. Don't do it.

Seller Will Not Have Guests Cancel and Rebook

When you execute the cancel-and-rebook method, the deposits are refunded to the guests, and when the guests rebook with you, their deposits are then repaid directly to you. When a seller refuses to do this, they've probably spent the deposits and do not have the money to refund the guests. This is a tough one to navigate. It's best to ask to have those deposit amounts held in an escrow account out of the seller's proceeds rather than to rely on the seller to provide a check at closing. It will take a little bit of fancy wording and amendment writing in order to make this work with the lender if you plan to use a vacation home loan, but it can be done.

A Note on Appraisals

Even though STRS are cash-flowing businesses when you purchase them, they are still residential properties (in most cases) and will need to be appraised as such. In other words, a residential property, in the eyes of an appraiser, is only worth what the sold residential comps in the area determine it is worth. It is not a commercial property; therefore, the amount of income that it brings in has no bearing on the appraisal value. It does have an indirect effect on the desirability of the property to investors and drives up what an investor might be willing to pay. However, if an investor is using conventional financing, such as a 10 percent down vacation home loan, to purchase an STR, the property is going to be appraised based on sold comps in the area. When a seller, or even a listing agent, tries to argue that a home is worth tens of thousands more than everything else on the market due to income, a great agent or an educated buyer will point out that the value of the property is determined by the appraiser based on sold comps, not income.

It's Not About Winning

Here's my last piece of advice regarding the contract process: Don't be your own worst enemy. It's not about the thrill of winning, or getting more from the seller than they are getting from you. It's about making the numbers work as an investment.

I once had a client who secured a great deal on a property where the cash-on-cash return was close to 50 percent. We made it through the inspection and appraisal contingencies and negotiated any repairs. About a week before closing, the buyer received a list of items that he would need to buy from his property management company. One of those items was bed linens. The buyer asked us if the bed linens would convey with the property, since the property was coming furnished. We explained to him that it is not customary for bed linens to convey, as they are usually owned by property management companies rather than sellers. This was laid out in the furniture agreement that was signed by both parties at the beginning of the contract process, but we pushed the listing side hard over the linens. The seller would not budge. The buyer sent several lengthy and very litigious emails regarding the bed linens, even threatening to sue for breach of contract, attorney fees, and "punitive damages." Since both sides were digging in their heels, I offered to pay for new sheets for the buyer. I didn't want him to lose out on a great deal over a few hundred dollars' worth of sheets. He refused, citing a matter of principle. He eventually walked away from the deal, and now some other investor is netting $50,000 a year because they were willing to buy a few sets of bedsheets and my buyer was not.

In another instance, a buyer made a well-below-asking-price offer on a property that was sure to get multiple offers. The buyer called me and said, "Tell the listing side if they don't have the property marked as pending in the next thirty minutes we will withdraw our offer." He was angry that the seller was waiting to see what other offers might come in. He was trying to force the seller to sell for a significant discount. Why would the seller care if he withdrew his low offer? The difference on the mortgage payment would have been nominal, and the cash flow would have been fantastic at either price. I tried to explain to my buyer that the only thing he would be doing by withdrawing the offer is guaranteeing that he wouldn't get the property. He withdrew the offer anyway, and the property sold for the asking price the same day.

It sounds silly, doesn't it—losing out on a great deal over inconsequential items? Undoubtedly those investors eventually regretted making decisions based on ego and competitiveness rather than ROI numbers. The lesson from these stories is this: Throughout the negotiation process, there will be periods of give-and-take between yourself and the seller. Emotions can run high during real estate deals, and it can be easy to fall into a power struggle and an "us versus them" mentality. But at the end of the day, it doesn't matter what is right or fair, or what you feel the seller should do or not do. The only thing that matters is whether the numbers work as an investment at the price for which you are able to get the property.

The purpose of real estate investing is not to decide who is the best at debating contract wording or who gets to walk away feeling like they "won" the negotiations. You win by making money on your property. In five years, you won't remember the negotiation, and you won't be proud of yourself for walking away from a great property because you didn't think the other party was being fair. You will be proud of yourself for the income stream you've been able to create and for all the great ways you have utilized that income to scale and create more generational wealth for yourself and your loved ones. Winning equals income, not feeling like you made the other guy concede the most.

Chapter 4

GENERAL STR ANALYSIS

Everyone can tell you the risk. An entrepreneur can see the reward.

—ROBERT KIYOSAKI

Once you've decided on a market, you'll need to know what to look for in a potential STR. The most important question to ask is: What type of property has the highest return? We will explore the answers to that question in this chapter.

RETAIL VERSUS OFF-MARKET

As investors, we have been indoctrinated to believe that if a property has hit the MLS, it's not a good investment. Many traditional investors think that the wholesalers pick off any real deals. If a property makes it past the wholesalers, then the listing agent will send it out to all of their investors, who will gobble it up if it has any value. This is not as true with STR properties as it is with traditional long-term investment properties.

For example, in metro markets, it's becoming more common for STR-eligible properties to be purpose-built new constructions, which are listed at the highest possible value in order to squeeze every dollar out of each one. In vacation markets, it's very difficult for the wholesaler model to work. Think about it: If a seller gets into financial trouble in a market where the majority of the properties being bought and sold are either true vacation homes or vacation rentals, they will unload those properties at retail prices well before they become "distressed" or before the seller has to accept any deep discounts on them. This is especially true of hot vacation rental markets where property values have appreciated significantly over the past decade.

The idea that any decent property will be gobbled up by real estate agents' investor lists is also a bit of a stretch. I have been an agent for years now, so I am going to take a liberty and make this statement: Many agents are dumb and/or lazy. In the case of real estate agents, the 98/2 rule applies. Only a handful of agents in any given market are going to know what an investor list is. Even fewer are going to have one, and even fewer are going to be proactive enough to use it for marketing. This, ladies and gentlemen, is why profitable STR properties make it to the MLS every day.

Still, it is possible to find off-market deals for STRs. One way is through local STR and real estate investing groups and their associated social media pages. Your choice of agent will also determine how much access you have to any off-market properties. You've already learned how to find and interview great agents. Use those tools to find one of the two percent of agents doing 98 percent of the work, and through them you will find any off-market deals available. An agent who does hundreds of deals with dozens of other agents a year is going to have the most connections and the greatest access to any premarket listings. But remember, off-market STRs are more like a dripping sink than a fountain. There will be an unsteady trickle of one or two at a time, and you'll have to act on them before they head down the drain. You'll need to be ready to analyze quickly and pounce if you come across one. Often the value of an off-market STR deal lies not in its lower price compared to its MLS counterparts. The real value of an off-market STR deal is the removal of the competition that comes with MLS properties.

Recently, the NAR passed a new policy called Clear Cooperation. This rule was enacted to give all agents access to every deal on the MLS and to prevent deals going only to the top-producing agents. Under this policy, all real estate agents have to post properties as active on the MLS within one business day, or forty-eight hours (whichever is shorter), of publicly marketing the property. The NAR defines "public marketing" as any email or communication about the property to anyone outside their own office. This regulation has impacted many agents' ability to provide off-market opportunities to their clients for any significant period of time, and it is something that we, as investors, need to be aware of. Some MLS boards have forms for sellers to sign that allow their agents to keep the property off-market for longer than the allotted one business day or forty-eight hours, but many do not. Unfortunately for us agents who do a lot of investor deals, we now have a limited amount of time to discuss off-market opportunities with our clients, so keep that in mind during your property search. If a property is off-market, you'll have to move fast!

SIZE DOES MATTER

Properties have different ROIs depending on size. As a general rule, properties with four bedrooms or more have higher ROIs and overall management efficiencies than their one- to three-bedroom counterparts. For example, I own 2 two-bedroom properties and 2 four-bedroom properties in the same market. My gross annual income on the four-bedroom properties is just over double the gross annual income on the two-bedrooms, but the expenses on the four-bedrooms are not double the expenses on the two-bedrooms. The expenses on the four-bedrooms are only about 15 percent higher than the expenses on the two-bedrooms, so my ROI on the four-bedrooms is significantly higher. Does that make my two-bedroom properties bad investments? No, it just makes the four-bedroom properties better.

While larger properties do have higher ROIs, if you only have enough capital for a smaller property, go ahead and pull that trigger to start generating some cash flow. In the amount of time it takes to accumulate a bigger down payment for a larger property, prices can rise so much that you miss other opportunities while saving.

DON'T REINVENT THE WHEEL

There are numerous Airbnb "gurus" out there who will charge you an arm and a leg to tell you to spend an extra $50,000 on your vacation rental in order to "set it apart" to maximize income. I can always tell when a client has been through one of these guru courses because they usually have some outrageous suggestions on what they should do with the property in order to augment cash flow.

In one instance, we were standing in a new-construction log cabin with custom fixtures, furniture, everything. It even had a putting green room already installed. The client then asked me if I had a contractor who could add "port holes" to the wall separating the putting green room and the game room. I asked him what he meant, and he said, "You know, port holes, like a cruise ship. And maybe a ball pit in this corner, and an indoor slide over there. And we will rip this floor out and put in a floor of pillows. It'll rent like crazy!"

A custom five-bedroom cabin with a view of the Great Smoky Mountains will rent like crazy the way it is, without going through all that time and expense. I asked him why he wanted to cut holes in brand-new, freshly stained Alpine log walls. "Oh, I went to Guru X's course, and he said you have to really set yourself apart. He has clients with full *Star Wars*–themed houses!" The client paid several thousand dollars for this person to tell him he needed to turn a beautiful cabin in the Great Smoky Mountains into a McDonald's PlayPlace in order to maximize ROI. Tourists come to the Great Smoky Mountains to rent cabins in the Great Smoky Mountains.

The point being: All you have to do is select a property that embodies the general expectation of tourists in the market. When tourists visit mountain areas, they just want a cabin. When tourists visit beach markets, they just want a nice condo or beach house. It is very easy to get caught up in over-improvements. Going too crazy with a community of tiny homes or tree houses or glamping structures (or whatever type of alternative property is featured on HGTV right now) treads a very fine line between a vanity project and an investment.

Speaking of which, the tiny homes, tree houses, glamping structures, and shipping container houses are all the rage, but I have yet to see anyone successfully execute these ideas. Even if they did, it would take a lot more time and resources than simply buying a property that fits the expectations of the market. You're an investor—just make the investment. There are no prizes for creativity, which brings me to my next point.

KEEP YOUR EMOTIONS OUT OF IT

Keeping your emotions out of LTR investments is easy. Keeping your emotions out of STR investments is harder. Why? Because they're fun. If you're searching in a beach or mountain market, you are bound to start picturing your family vacationing or spending holidays in the property. Do your absolute best to keep thoughts like this at bay. As soon as you allow your emotions—and, in turn, your personal preferences—to creep into your decision making, your ROI can decrease before you even make the offer. It comes down to the basic rule of keeping business and pleasure separate. If you try to combine the two, your income will suffer because you'll want to use the property for your own purposes. Just focus on what rents the best. Keep your investor mindset and analysis—not your desire to impress your friends with your cool beach house—at the forefront when making investment decisions.

GROSS MEANS GROSS

STR investors have different opinions of what "gross income" means or should include when quoting rental history. Many will say gross should include only price per night and should disregard cleaning fees or taxes. Some say that gross should include taxes but not cleaning fees. I call these numbers "hybrid gross" numbers. So what's the right answer? "Gross" means "all monies coming in." Therefore, in my opinion, cleaning fees should always be included in gross numbers because there is income built into the cleaning fees. I call these "true gross" numbers. Many STR investors charge their guests a significantly higher cleaning fee than what they are charged by their housekeepers. For example, a housekeeper charges $100 per cleaning, the owner charges a $150 cleaning fee to the guests, and the property is cleaned an average of five times per month. That extra $50 per cleaning adds up to $3,000 in income per year. Why is that $3,000 not allowed to count toward gross income? Those who believe it shouldn't count are missing out on a significant piece of income.

Another reason why true gross, and not hybrid gross, needs to be quoted is that most online booking platforms send homeowners a 1099 at the end of the year. These 1099s are based on true gross income. In other words, when analyzing an STR, it's important to know the true gross income because Uncle Sam is going to expect his cut of the true gross, not hybrid gross, at the end of the year.

Chapter 5

ANALYZING YOUR POTENTIAL STR PROPERTY

The best model to follow is 'nothing ventured, nothing gained.'

—RICHARD BRANSON, "LOSING MY VIRGINITY:
HOW I'VE SURVIVED, HAD FUN, AND MADE
A FORTUNE DOING BUSINESS MY WAY"

DETERMINING INCOME POTENTIAL

There are a lot of black-and-white, hard-and-fast metrics out there used to determine whether a property will make sense as a long-term investment: 10 percent cap rate or over, the 1 percent rule... the list goes on. LTR numbers fit nicely into spreadsheets with assigned values and very little variability. The ROI of an STR, however, depends heavily upon a number of subjective and unquantifiable variables.

With STRs, income potential will always be a range rather than an exact number. An underperforming property is almost never underperforming because of the property itself, but because of poor management. Therefore, with STR analysis, we put together a number of data points from several sources (some of which were mentioned in Chapter Two) to come up with a reasonable income range within which a property can be expected to perform. We will discuss the different variables and data point sources over the next few pages.

Data Point 1: Rental History

The number one rule when evaluating the income potential of a specific property is to never take rental history at face value. When I speak with new investors regarding STR numbers, many have already been scouring Zillow for properties in the market they are considering investing in. They sometimes say things like, "I'm having trouble making the numbers work." My first question to them is always: "Where are those rental numbers coming from?" In almost every instance, they're from the Zillow rental history.

Thomas Edison reputedly said, "Opportunity is missed by most people because it is dressed in overalls and looks like hard work." The biggest mistake an investor can possibly make in an STR analysis is to stop their analysis at the rental history they're given. The property with the low rental history is the opportunity wearing overalls—since "low" can be defined differently among investors.

What I am about to say is going to sound crazy to your investor brain, but stay with me: Rental history means nothing, and in some cases, it can be the absolute poorest indicator of a property's potential. Rental history is a variable that should be used as one data point for your analysis, not the benchmark. Put on the overalls and do the work to analyze how you can improve the rental numbers on an underperforming property. Would you walk away from a good multifamily LTR deal because you knew the manager was charging less than market rent? Absolutely not! Don't walk away from an STR based on low rental numbers garnered by one random manager. Always analyze further.

Different property managers can manage two identical properties and produce wildly different numbers based upon their skill, marketing, and style of management. In many cases—especially in mature vacation rental markets where management companies have been around since the 1980s and '90s—low production numbers from the local, or older, property managers are common.

Back in the day, before STRs were a viable investment strategy, vacation home owners were forced to utilize the services of local property managers. There was no Vrbo or Airbnb—local managers were the only option for owners in these markets. Many of these old-school property management companies refuse to utilize the technology that is putting them out of business: the major online booking platforms. They rely solely on direct bookings through their stand-alone websites.

Some local property management companies are openly hostile toward this shift in booking preferences. I have been on conference calls with property managers who will flat-out tell clients, "You'll never make any money on Airbnb and Vrbo, which is why you need our company to professionally manage your rental at a rate of 30 percent of your gross income." This business model hurts properties' performance because as of 2020, about 90 percent of tourists go straight to their online platform of choice to book travel from their smartphone. The ease of booking accommodations in any city, anywhere in the world, directly from a smartphone will always win out against loyalty to property management companies.

Because these property managers are not properly utilizing the technology necessary to keep up with the industry, their performance numbers are going to be significantly lower. Also, just because a property is listed by a management company on the major booking platforms, it does not mean the listing is being utilized and booked. In some cases, these managers have what I call "dummy listings" posted on the major booking platforms to advertise to potential clients. However, these listings will usually have significant processing fees tacked on at the end of the booking process. This is their attempt to drive guests to book directly on the property management's website instead.

The second STR property I ever purchased—a very sweet mom-and-pop cabin managed by a rental company—had a rental history of $23,000 for the previous year. My first year with it, we were able to gross $45,000. We didn't change one stitch of furniture or add any amenities. We literally just posted our listings where the tourist traffic is: major booking platforms. It does not always require any experience or resources to improve upon past rental history—just a willingness to take a few extra steps in your analysis. Never stop your analysis at the rental numbers. Also analyze the management.

Data Point 2: STR-Specific Data Companies

We briefly touched on STR-specific data companies in Chapter Two, where we covered choosing a market. More options are surfacing online all the time, but AirDNA, Mashvisor, and Key Data are currently the big players in the STR data market. Sign up for a subscription to as many of these companies as you like—there is no such thing as too much data.

Pay more attention to the aggregate data, or the overall trends for properties similar to yours in the market. Many of these services offer property-specific analyzers and projections. While those functions can be a lot of fun, try to stay away from them. All they do is shrink the data sample to the few properties closest to the subject, and if there are any outliers in the immediate vicinity, the analyzer tool will pick them out and skew the projection. You want to keep the data sample as large as possible so that outliers have less of an effect on the numbers.

Data Point 3: Major Property Management Company Projections

Depending on the market you're in, there will be a number of property management companies you can call on for rental projections. When obtaining rental projections, stay away from mom-and-pop companies and utilize data only from companies you've vetted and determined are up-to-date on all available marketing and rental channels. The three biggest are Vacasa, Evolve, and TurnKey. Because of their size, these companies will have access to plenty of proprietary data and analysis tools that will give you a more accurate projection.

Data Point 4: The Enemy Method

The Enemy Method is a quick grassroots way to analyze a property. There are five steps to the Enemy Method:

1. Log on to the online booking platform you'll be using to rent your property.
2. Zoom in on the area or neighborhood where you plan to purchase a property.
3. Find a similar property (same number of bedrooms and general features) that is being managed in the same way you plan to manage yours (self-managed or using a particular property manager) with a lot of reviews (preferably more than a hundred).
4. Review the price per night, calendar occupancy, housekeeping fee,

minimum- and maximum-night stay, house rules, pet policies, and so on.

5. Determine how your potential property listing can outperform this listing. Does it have high-quality professional photos, or did the owner take dark cell phone shots? Does the listing use poor grammar or have subpar descriptions of the property?

Once you have reviewed your neighbors' listings, you should have a pretty good idea of how you should market your property on the site.

Now that you've accumulated a few data points, it's time to start your analysis. To ensure that you're truly comparing apples to apples, use the same tool or metric to analyze all the properties you are considering. Do not use previous rental history to analyze one property and rental projection to analyze another. You must measure all properties by the same yardstick.

DETERMINING EXPENSES

One of the biggest differences between LTR and STR investing is the expenses paid by the owner. With LTRs, the tenant usually pays for utilities; with STRs, the owner usually pays. Below is a list of expenses STR owners can generally expect to pay:

1. Electricity
2. Cable/internet
3. Water
4. Gas
5. HOA fees (some HOAs will include utilities or cable and internet in their fees, so be careful not to have two line items that cover the same costs)
6. Cleaning fees (while this is a pass-through expense to guests, it is still an expense that is deducted from your true gross)
7. Maintenance
8. Landscaping/pest control

Market-Specific Expenses

Some markets will have expenses that are particular to that area. For example, most properties in the Great Smoky Mountains market are on well water rather than city water. The best way to locate expenses, or "cost to own," is to have your agent reach out to the listing agent to obtain that information from the seller. The seller should be able to provide a detailed list of utility expenses and other costs to own the property. Your agent should also be able to provide ballpark costs for general and one-time maintenance fees in that market, such as septic pumping, well pump replacement, and pool and hot tub maintenance.

Insurance

Regular homeowners or LTR insurance does not cover all the scenarios that can possibly arise when it comes to STR investing. To be sure of what you need, speak with an insurance professional to find a specific policy for you. In general, the main options for STR insurance are:

1. **STR-specific insurance policies.** STR-specific insurance companies focus solely on supplying insurance to STR owners and investors. The premiums are typically more expensive than other types of insurance. However, policies tend to be comprehensive and cover a number of scenarios that other types of insurance will not cover, such as bedbug remediation and lost income due to the shutdown of a property during bedbug remediation.

2. **STR riders on homeowners policies.** Many traditional homeowners insurance providers now offer STR rider options that can be added to an existing policy.

3. **Commercial umbrella policies.** These policies provide additional liability protection beyond the liability coverage limits of other policies to help cover costs beyond the standard insurance claim, such as legal fees and medical bills. It's not a bad idea to have an umbrella policy in addition to any other policies you choose for your STRs.

Flood Insurance

If you plan to buy in a beach market, familiarize yourself with flood insurance. Depending on the exact location of the property, you may or may not require it. Take a look at the Federal Emergency Management Agency (FEMA) flood maps online, and talk with local insurance providers to get the best information on flood zones and how they are insured.

One specific insurance in coastal markets relates to the CBRA (often called "cobra") zone. Essentially, the U.S. Fish and Wildlife Service utilizes CBRA zones to prohibit new development or modification of coastal barriers. Depending on a number of factors, some properties in CBRA zones, which can be found at www.fws.gov, are eligible for federal flood insurance at a reasonable cost. Others will not be covered and will require private flood insurance that meets the CBRA zone qualifications. There are very few underwriters that provide private CBRA zone insurance.

PUTTING THE PIECES TOGETHER: ANALYZING DEALS

When choosing an STR investment, the most important part of your analysis should be purchase price versus income—or, to take it a step further, the amount of cash income earned on the amount of cash invested in the deal. This is known as the cash-on-cash return.

Cash-on-Cash Return

Cash-on-cash (CoC) return is the name of the game with STR investing. In other words, what is the amount of money you are putting in versus the amount of money you are getting out at the end of the year? Subtract the expenses from the income. Is that number enough to justify the amount of money you are putting down to acquire the property? If yes, proceed. If no, keep looking.

While there is no hard-and-fast benchmark for CoC return in STR investing, anything above 20 percent CoC is considered a good deal. However, I have seen clients hit well into the 40–50 percent range and even higher. Keep in mind, though, that the CoC return can be easily manipulated based on the type of loan you choose. A 10 percent down vacation home loan will yield a higher CoC than a traditional investment loan or a commercial loan, so make sure you factor your loan type into your analysis. Below is an example of how to calculate the CoC return on a $500,000 property utilizing a 20 percent down, thirty-year fixed conventional mortgage:

Purchase price: $500,000
Down payment: $100,000 (cash invested)
Gross annual income: $75,000
Expenses (utilities, cleaning, etc.): $25,538

$$\text{\$75,000 gross annual income} - \text{\$25,538 expenses} = \text{\$49,462 net operating income (NOI)}$$

$$\text{\$49,462 NOI} - \text{\$22,224 annual mortgage, taxes, and insurance escrowed} = \text{\$27,238 cash flow}$$

CoC return:

$$\left(\frac{27{,}238 \text{ cash flow}}{100{,}000 \text{ cash invested}} \right) \times 100 = 27.238 \text{ CoC return}$$

Gross Rent Multiplier

Another metric commonly used when investing in STRs is the gross rent multiplier (GRM). GRM is the ratio of a property's price to its gross rental income. It is calculated by dividing the market value or purchase price of a property by the gross rental income. The GRM is often used by investors to determine how many years it will take to pay off a property. Let's take the above $500,000 property for example:

Purchase price: $500,000
Gross rental income: $75,000
$500,000 purchase price ÷ $75,000 gross rental income = 6.67 GRM

In STR investing, as a quick-and-easy method of analysis, we often use a derivative of the GRM by expressing the gross annual income as a percentage of the purchase price. For example:

Purchase price: $500,000
Gross annual income: $75,000
Income as a percentage of purchase price: 15 percent

Any property that grosses above 10 percent of the purchase price is considered a base hit and worth a possible purchase. Anything above 15 percent is a triple, and 20 percent is considered a home run and a deal that is not to be passed up. GRM and its derivative calculations are quick and easy methods of analysis, but they do not take any expenses into account, so it's important to build a pro forma in order to determine the expenses and net income of a potential property.

Pro Formas

I can't speak for all markets, but in those in which I operate, most sellers will not provide a pro forma to prospective buyers. The sellers may not even be familiar with the term "pro forma." In order to adequately analyze a deal in any market, you'll need to learn how to build your own.

A good STR pro forma will include cleaning fees, property management fees (if you aren't self-managing), occupancy taxes, maintenance fees, and all utilities paid by the owner of the property. In some markets, it's standard for a "cost to own" sheet to be provided. In other markets, it's called a "utilities disclosure." This document will provide you with the average electricity, water, cable and internet, and HOA fees that the seller has paid monthly throughout the duration of their ownership.

In some markets, utilities and expense information will not be provided. Ask your real estate agent if that is standard in the market you're exploring. If there are no expenses or utilities disclosures, you can sometimes call the local electric company to get an idea of the average monthly bill for a property of the size you are looking at. Use the Enemy Method to gather average handyperson call fees, as well as standard cleaning fees for properties in your target size range.

Capital expenditures (CapEx) will range between 1 and 3 percent. On a brand-new construction, you'll have few, if any, CapEx items in your first year or two, but on a twenty-year-old build, you might spend the full 3 percent. Use your own judgment to determine what percentage you want to use for CapEx items in your analysis.

SAMPLE SELF-MANAGED SHORT-TERM-RENTAL PRO FORMA, 4-BEDROOM PURCHASE PRICE $650,000

Gross Annual Income — $95,750

Gross means all monies coming in, including: nightly rental rate, cleaning fees, and local occupancy tax. State sales tax is paid separately by booking platforms and therefore is not included on pro forma.

Booking Fees — −$2,872.50

Cleaning Fees — −$7,500

Calculated at an average of 5 cleans per month at a set per-clean rate (this number is an average and will be less for larger properties). This range includes laundry, trash disposal, etc. Keep in mind that most hosts charge the guest $20–$50 more than what they are charged by their cleaner.

Occupancy Tax — -$2,633.13

Occupancy tax will vary slightly depending on whether the property is within or outside of city limits, but the average is ~2.75% of gross annual income.

Property Tax — −$3,500

Electricity — −$3,600

Assuming electric heat and electric appliances (rather than gas)

Water — −$575

Cable and Internet — −$1,500

This number assumes the cost of traditional cable with cable boxes. It can be reduced by using only Internet streaming services.

Insurance — −$3,100

Insurance rates will vary depending upon the company and type of policy. Be sure to shop around for the best rate.

Miscellaneous Maintenance — −$2,250

Calculated at an average rate of $75/maintenance person call, at 30 calls per year

Total Operating Expenses — $27,530.63

NOI — $68,219.37

These numbers are good faith estimates and are in no way guaranteed. Performance will depend solely on ownership and management. Only monthly fees are shown in these proformas, and they do not account for one-time expenses and CapEx items. Copyright The Short Term Shop.

The most important advice I can close out this chapter with is: Be adaptable. There are many moving parts and intangible elements that determine the financial success of an STR. While it's important to focus on the numbers, they're not the whole story when it comes to analysis. So if you're going to spend hours agonizing over a data error in cell C27 of a spreadsheet rather than looking at the bigger picture, STR investing may not be for you.

PART 2
SELF-MANAGING YOUR STR REMOTELY

Chapter 6

DO I NEED A PROPERTY MANAGER?

You're living in the past, it's a new generation.

—JOAN JETT, "BAD REPUTATION"

One of the biggest decisions investors must make before purchasing an STR is whether to use a property management company. The idea that a property manager is necessary for a successful out-of-state investment is an antiquated one. If you *want* a property manager, that's fine. Do you *need* a property manager if you invest out of state? No. There are certainly situations in which professional property management can be useful, but if you're interested in turbocharging your cash flow and bootstrapping to scale into more doors as quickly as possible, self-management is the only option. If you're ready to get started, here are a few FAQs regarding self-management.

1. **Who will meet guests to grant them access?** A simple Wi-Fi door lock system eliminates the need for anyone to meet guests at the property to exchange keys or let them into the building.
2. **What if something breaks?** If a toilet breaks in the property, you call a plumber, just as you would for your primary residence. It doesn't matter whether the property is down the street or 3,000 miles away—the course of action for coordinating repairs is the same. Anything in the world can be handled with a phone call, email, or text message. No repair requires you to be present at the property.
3. **Will I be bothered in the middle of the night all the time?** No. Will it happen at some point? If you own enough properties for a long enough time, of course it will. Though it most definitely will not happen all the time. The inconvenience of receiving a few middle-of-the-night calls over the course of your life as an STR investor is far outweighed by the wealth you will have added to your family's income stream.
4. **What do I do if there is an emergency and I live too far away to get there quickly?** What constitutes an emergency? Property damage? A fire? A flood? A guest having a heart attack in your living room? If you're not a first responder, the chances of your presence improving an emergency situation are slim. Let the professionals do their jobs; all you can do is make the relevant phone calls. Beyond that, there's no reason to get involved.

Managing an STR amounts to answering a few texts and phone calls a week. In fact, with the right tools and automations, it should take you about thirty minutes a week to manage one property. There is nothing a property management company does that an owner cannot do right from their smartphone, other than suck all the cash flow out of the deal.

THE CASE FOR SELF-MANAGEMENT

The average cost for property management of an STR is 20–30 percent of the gross income of the property and can reach up to 40 percent in certain markets. The average net profit that a mortgaged STR can expect after expenses and the mortgage payment is between 35 and 50 percent of the gross. Knock off another 20 or 30 percent, and it's pretty darn difficult to bring in a substantial cash flow. In some markets you might even be in negative-cash-flow territory after management fees.

WHEN TO USE A PROPERTY MANAGER

Despite the high cost, there is a time and place for STR property management companies. In my opinion, property managers can be great options in the following two scenarios::
1. When you, as an investor, are no longer bootstrapping to roll the income into more properties and scale as quickly as possible.
2. When cash flow is not your number one priority.

If you've scaled your STR business to upwards of ten units and you're happy with the total number of doors in your real estate portfolio, putting it on cruise control can make more sense than self-managing to squeeze every dollar out of your properties. Also, if you're planning to use your property as a part-time vacation home rather than a full-time investment, there may not be much point in self-managing. The same applies if you're just trying to break even (though if this is your goal, you're probably not on your way to financial independence as a real estate investor).

There are a number of fantastic STR managers out there, but this book is about how to manage your own STR. Therefore, the primary focus of the next chapter will be to teach you the basics of self-management.

Chapter 7
BUILDING YOUR TEAM

The team, not the individual, is the ultimate champion.

—MIA HAMM, "GO FOR THE GOAL"

Any investor—even someone with a day job or children or other obligations and responsibilities—can easily self-manage an STR. In fact, you can manage an STR from anywhere in the world in less than one hour per week. There are American expat clients who manage their STRs in the United States from China. There are military clients who manage their STRs in the United States while being deployed in Afghanistan. You just need to get the right team and systems in place. (If you're having a difficult time with the concept of self-managing an STR remotely, check out the book *Who Not How: The Formula to Achieve Bigger Goals Through Accelerating Teamwork* by Dan Sullivan and Benjamin Hardy. While it's not about STRs specifically, it will get you thinking differently about delegating tasks and trusting others to perform them.)

To get started, you'll need two core team members: your housekeeper and your handyperson. Once you have hired those two, they will be able to recommend any other vendors you may need. For example, your cleaner is likely going to know a handyperson, your handyperson should be able to suggest a plumber, and so on.

In many markets, it can be difficult to find reliable vendors with just a quick Google search. Try these sites instead:

1. Market-specific STR-owner Facebook groups
2. Facebook Marketplace
3. Thumbtack
4. Angi (formerly Angie's List) and HomeAdvisor
5. Airbnb, Vrbo, and the other major online booking platforms.

Another way to find a housekeeper is to introduce yourself to your neighbors and politely ask if they have someone they could recommend. Other STR owners might not want to share this information for fear their cleaners will no longer have time to adequately service their own properties, but all you need is for one neighbor to show enough kindness to give you their housekeeper's contact information.

HOUSEKEEPERS

Once you get the names of a few housekeepers, start making some phone calls. The best time to interview potential housekeepers is after you close. If you can't wait until closing, at least hold off until the inspection and appraisal contingencies have been satisfied. That way you won't waste the housekeeper's time, since they can't give a quote on a hypothetical property. Your cleaner is absolutely the most important person to the success of your STR. A good housekeeper is worth their weight in gold, and you should treat them accordingly. The more properties you have, the easier it will be to find a good cleaner. When you have 10 properties' worth of potential income to offer, housekeepers will make it a priority to speak with you. But when you are a newbie with one property, things will be a bit more difficult because you are not swinging a very big hammer... yet.

Housekeeping Interview Tips

Almost anyone can clean a house, but the key is to make sure the housekeeper has a reliable communication style and is a good personality fit.

You can expect to end up firing a housekeeper or two before finding your long-term housekeeping team member, and that's okay.

When I first started, I was 27 years old, and my housekeeper, who had been in the STR cleaning business for more than a decade, was in her 50s. We made it through six months—a crucial six months that I am grateful for because it got our business off the ground. However, I was a newbie and made a few communication mistakes, and I was never able to regain control of the relationship. From the very first booking, I let her steamroll me because I was nervous and afraid to lose her. She called me in a tizzy after the first checkout and said she would need extra money because the guests were so outrageously messy. Assuming it was my fault for booking a bad guest, I very eagerly obliged.

Over time, these phone calls became more frequent. When we began our relationship, we had agreed upon a per-cleaning price, not an hourly rate. While I wanted to make sure she was adequately compensated for any extra work outside the normal scope, I was eventually paying an hourly wage for a per-cleaning rate.

I hired my handyman to take a few videos directly after checkout on two occasions so that I could see the condition in which the guests had left the property. Both times the property was in great condition, but both times the cleaner called me complaining about how out-of-control messy it was. At this point, I had to let her go. It wasn't her fault—it was mine for not controlling the situation from the outset. She did a great job, and several of my colleagues and friends still use her to this day. But I did not set clear expectations and boundaries, so I paid the price.

Finally, you have to ask for references. A housekeeper should be able to provide the names of two or three happy customers who would be willing to speak with you.

Negotiating Price and Duties

There are two general setups for cleaners and pricing:

1. The housekeeper will charge a certain rate just to clean the property, and the owner will provide all of the items to be restocked—toilet paper, paper products, dishwashing detergent, etc.
2. The housekeeper will charge a higher per-cleaning rate but will take care of all restocking items.

The first approach allows the owner to have more control over the quality of items (no scratchy toilet paper!) and keep detailed cost spreadsheets for their records. If a guest ever has a question about anything, I know exactly what is in the house. With this method, the cleaner lets the owner know when a certain item needs to be restocked, and the owner orders it online to be shipped directly to the cleaner's home.

The second approach is more hands-off for the owner but is subject to the availability of items at the cleaner's local store. Owners and housekeepers will need to agree upon brands up front, or the owner will need to be flexible and allow the housekeeper to make decisions about what to purchase. Neither approach is incorrect—it just depends on your comfort level and the type of relationship you have with your housekeeper.

How to Pay the Housekeeper—and How Often

After you hire a cleaner (or any vendor, for that matter), they will have to fill out a W-9 before they can begin working and get paid. Next, discuss the best way to pay them. Housekeepers often prefer online payment systems like Venmo. However, in order to keep it legal and bookkeeping-friendly, you'll have to pay them through direct deposit or a legal online invoice payment platform funded by your designated business bank account. Invoices are the key here.

Payment frequency can differ from market to market. Some housekeepers will want to be paid after every cleaning. This can be an efficient method in markets where stays are longer (such as beach markets) but cumbersome in markets where stays average between two and five days. Other cleaners will send a monthly invoice to be paid at the end of each month.

My preference is to pay every other week. That way the cleaners are paid consistently without inconvenience, and the payments are not spaced so far apart that the housekeeper needs advances in order to buy cleaning products or pay employees. Whatever you work out with your housekeeper, ensure the payments are trackable for tax purposes at the end of the year. Receiving proper invoices from the housekeeper is ideal, though emails can suffice in most cases. I find that the PayPal invoicing platform is the most efficient and easiest way to track when a housekeeper does not have a bookkeeper or a robust bookkeeping platform.

Tips for Keeping an Eye on Cleaner Performance

If your property is not clean enough, your guests will always let you know. It could be sparkling clean, and you'll still get a guest who moves appliances out from the wall to find dirt to point out to you.

I'm often asked how out-of-state investors can keep an eye on cleaning performance. One way, as mentioned earlier, is to hire your handyman or a gig worker from an app like Thumbtack to take photos for you after the cleaner leaves. Another strategy that has worked well for me is to pick one guest each month and ask them to let you know if anything is not clean enough. Most guests are happy to provide this feedback, and it's a quick and easy way to spot-check your housekeeper.

The absolute biggest fear and worst-case scenario for any STR owner is a missed cleaning, which leads to a guest checking in to a property and finding the previous guest's dirty sheets and trash. This is a hazard of the business. I would love to tell you there's a way to prevent this from ever happening, but there isn't. Over the course of your STR ownership, you'll deal with this at least once. Here are steps you can take to minimize guest dissatisfaction in case of a missed cleaning:

1. **Keep a set of clean sheets and towels in a closet.** This way, if your housekeeper has to rush over on short notice, they won't have to waste time at their home or laundry facility gathering sheets and towels for your unit.

2. **Find a local restaurant that will allow you to pay for your guests' dinner over the phone.** Guest check-in is typically in the afternoon, and in the rare event that a cleaning is missed, you can suggest that they leave their luggage and head to dinner on you. When they get back, their unit will be clean. An alternative would be to purchase gift cards to local restaurants and keep them hidden at the property for guests to use in these instances.

3. **Don't be too hard on your housekeeper for a missed cleaning.** Unless it happens frequently (in which case, you need to find a new housekeeper), don't blast them for one mistake. They are human and miscommunications happen. As long as they make every effort to rush over to the property and clean it immediately, treat them with grace. You need your cleaner to be happy and to want to do a great job for you!

A Final Note on Cleaning

When you purchase an STR that was previously a rental, it's going to need a deep cleaning. Don't panic if, right before closing, a cleaner quotes you $1,200 for a three-day cleaning job. It's a shock and you might worry you've made a mistake by purchasing the property, but it's okay! A dirty property is a reflection of poor management, not a bad property. Get the place cleaned up and ready to be run properly.

HANDYPEOPLE

The second-most-important member of your team is your handyperson. If your agent does not have any recommendations, your cleaner will probably have a few. Best practice is to have several handypeople on your list. Try to rotate them for nonemergency jobs so that you maintain a good rapport with all of them. That way, when a situation does arise that needs immediate attention, you have several reliable options at the ready.

What Do They Charge?

Most handypeople will charge a call fee and an hourly rate on top of that for larger jobs. For example, my handyman charges me $50 per call out to the property. If it's a quick and simple fix, like a leak, he won't charge me on top of the call fee. If it's something more time-consuming, like replacing a toilet in order to fix the leak, he will charge me an hourly rate plus materials on top of the call fee.

A NOTE ABOUT VENDORS AND MICROMANAGEMENT

No vendor is perfect. At one point or another, a vendor is going to tick you off. Once, I sent my handyman out to check a leaky tub in a unit. He charged me $75 for the trip and assessed that there was nothing wrong. After a guest checked out, my cleaner sent me a photo of where they had used the leaky tub. Not only was there a leak—it was a big one. The ceiling below it had a big wet spot, as did the bed and carpet in the room underneath. When I called my handyman to reassess the leak, he said he wouldn't be able to visit the property until the following day. While I was terribly annoyed, I simply called the next handyman on my list, and he fixed the problem before my next guests checked in later that afternoon.

The takeaway here is that when things go wrong with vendors (and they will), don't freak out and question your whole reason for investing in STRs in the first place. Keep your head high, solve the problem, and go back to your day.

In a similar vein, don't micromanage your vendors. That's one of the best ways to lower your cash flow. You must be able to roll with the punches and be adaptable. Rigidity will get you nowhere in STR investing.

I've only ever had one client out of hundreds fail at STR investing, and it was due to her management style. She micromanaged her way through dozens of independent cleaners as well as cleaning companies. No answer or repair was ever good enough for her. Ultimately, her downfall was micromanaging her guests, which we will discuss in a later chapter. Moral of the story: Micromanaging equals stress; flexibility and adaptability equal maximized cash flow.

Chapter 8

BUILDING YOUR LISTING

Make it simple. Make it memorable. Make it inviting to look at.

—LEO BURNETT

What platforms should you use to market your property? It depends. At the time of this writing, there are two categories of STR listing sites:

1. Airbnb/Vrbo
2. The rest of the online travel agencies (OTAs)

AIRBNB/VRBO

If you're looking for the most streamlined process, your best bet is to post your listing on Airbnb and Vrbo, as these sites are easy to sync with each other and compatible with most channel management platforms (which we'll discuss later). Here are a few other items to note about each platform:

1. **Price:** Airbnb charges a 3 percent booking fee on every booking. Vrbo gives hosts two options: a $499 per year subscription or a 5 percent pay-per-booking fee.
2. **Interface:** While the apps themselves are very similar, the Airbnb app is a bit more streamlined and user-friendly than Vrbo's.
3. **Security deposits:** Vrbo charges a refundable damage deposit to the guest's credit card, whereas Airbnb just places a hold on the funds and does not charge the card unless the host files a damage claim.
4. **Tax/fee collection:** Airbnb will collect and remit state sales and local occupancy tax on behalf of owners in most states, while Vrbo requires owners to remit those taxes themselves.
5. **Customer service calls:** You generally won't need to call either platform's customer service line unless something has gone wrong, but treat every call as an opportunity to learn how to better handle a situation the next time it comes up. Take notes or record calls so that you can become more adept at troubleshooting issues, learn how to navigate the hierarchy of customer service reps, and figure out which contacts will be able to most effectively resolve your issues. A few common reasons why owners would need to call customer service are app glitches, calendar and booking issues, and in some cases, disputes with guests.

THE REST OF THE OTAS

There are a handful of other OTAs where STR investors can post their listings to solicit bookings. Some of the better-known ones are:
1. Booking.com
2. Tripadvisor
3. FlipKey
4. Hotels.com

Each of these OTAs will have different pricing structures and fees. My properties in all three of my markets stay so booked using only Airbnb and Vrbo that I don't complicate my process by using any other platforms.

DIRECT BOOKINGS

There is a growing movement of #bookdirect STR owners out there who do not use any listing platforms. They rely instead on social media and their own independent websites to book their properties. This method is pretty time-consuming and requires a lot of extra tools (website design and hosting, graphic design, copywriting, social media advertising, SEO, payment processing, calendar software; the list goes on). Many owners prefer to manage their property this way, as they have full control over any and all booking policies. But if you're a real estate investor who wants to streamline the process as much as possible, an independent booking website may not be the most efficient option. Nonetheless, there are several advantages to direct bookings:

1. You'll save money on platform fees and commissions.
2. You'll have more control over cancellation and refund policies.
3. You'll be able to offer more competitive pricing to your guests since you'll be saving money on platform fees and commissions.
4. If you use this method correctly, your STR income will not be dependent on any third-party platforms.

There are several websites and templates available for investors who prefer to acquire more direct bookings so they don't have to rely on the rules and regulations of the major booking platforms. These sites include booking engines, secure payment processors, and customer-facing websites.

WHAT SHOULD MY LISTING INCLUDE?

Listing Photos

The best marketing tool for any property in any market is professional photos. The better the photos, the more clicks your listing will attract; the more clicks your listing attracts, the more bookings you will receive. Make sure you have bright interior photos, excellent exterior photos that clearly represent what the property and its surroundings look like, and drone photos. Some investors don't want to spend the money on drone shots, but they really do make a listing stand out. Guests like to see what the area immediately surrounding a property looks like, and drone photos do a great job of displaying that. They can also be used to create maps with arrows showing how close attractions and restaurants are to the property. Other items you may want to take photos of include open cabinets and drawers, so guests know what your kitchen is stocked with before booking, and a screenshot of your internet speed for guests who plan to work remotely or stream videos.

One investor tried to get by with smartphone photos they took during the inspection. In their listing photos, you could see the reflection of the owner in the bathroom mirrors, as well as the inspector bent over a toilet. That property easily could have produced an extra $10,000 a year had the photos not been so sloppy. Investors, stick to investing and hire a professional photographer for your listing photos. You will not regret it.

Listing Copy

The goal of your listing copy is not only to provide a description of the property to attract renters, but also to prevent you from answering the same ten questions over and over for the rest of your life.

First, your listing should include a vibrant description of the property. Make sure to use proper grammar and spelling to look professional. If you don't feel comfortable writing the property description, hire a copywriter. Describe the property in detail, including how many beds and pull-out couches are available for sleeping. List any amenities that guests might find appealing—the privacy of the back deck, size of the televisions, brand of the cookware—and anything they might not. The worst thing that can happen is for a guest to arrive and be unpleasantly surprised by something. Steep roads, no internet, a messy neighbor— you may think that mentioning these items in the description will scare guests away, but if you have bought in the right market and word these things properly, most guests will not be bothered by them.

For example, I have a property that is on a terrifying road. Instead of focusing on the negative, I describe it this way: "The road up to this secluded mountain cabin was used by loggers in the early 1900s to haul timber from the top of the mountain to the bottom. It's paved in some places and gravel in some places. It might make you a little nervous on your first trip up, but once you do it a few times, you'll be a total mountain pro!" Because of this description, guests almost never mention the road in our reviews, and if they do, they say something like, "The road is steep, but the hosts let us know beforehand, so we were prepared." That's more of a compliment to us as hosts for setting proper expectations than it is a complaint about the road. To summarize: Disclose, disclose, disclose, but put a positive spin on it!

Your listing should also include a list of the most visited attractions, as well as the distance from your property to each of them, because guests always ask. Additionally, it helps to make a list of all restaurants and grocery stores in the area that deliver to your property.

Perhaps the most important part of your listing copy is your house rules and guest expectations. Do not neglect this section! This is where you'll put the obvious things like no smoking inside, quiet hours, rules for any amenities, fireplace usage, and so on. It's also where you'll list your pet policy.

Whether to Be Pet-Friendly

Many travelers look for pet-friendly accommodations, and pet fees equal extra income, but accepting pets can result in additional expenses and headaches for both owner and cleaner. While being pet-friendly sounds like a great idea, all it takes is one person bringing a big, white shedding dog to change everything.

When I bought my first STR, I wanted to be pet-friendly. For one, I am a gigantic animal lover. I also travel with my dog, so I usually rent pet-friendly accommodations. I've found that these accommodations often smell like dog from the second I walk in, and I have come to expect that. It comes with the territory. However, guests who do not travel with dogs are generally not thrilled with the smell of previous canine visitors. The only way to guarantee that a property will never smell like pets is to make it non-pet-friendly. In our case, our listing stayed pet-friendly for exactly three pet stays. It was not worth the pet fee. It took our housekeeper four hours to remove the dog hair that had accumulated in every corner and piece of fabric in the house after each stay—not the best way to keep your cleaner happy.

While we are on the subject, at some point in your STR-owning career, a guest is going to tell you that their Yorkie or Pomeranian is an emotional support animal, or ESA. There are many places online where pets can be certified as an ESA for a few bucks, even though they have no training or "job" like a true service animal. Read up on and familiarize yourself with the current Americans with Disabilities Act (ADA) guidelines on what constitutes a true service animal versus an ESA. The ADA requires you to allow service animals—it's discriminatory not to—but ESAs are not service animals, so you are not required to grant a stay to a guest with an ESA.

Minimum- and Maximum-Night Stays

When setting up your listing, you'll need to determine a minimum- and maximum-night stay. What is considered standard will differ from market to market, but keep one thing in mind: The lower your minimum-night stay, the higher the potential for your occupancy rate. If you set a four-night minimum, you'll have a lot of one- to three-night holes in your calendar. If you set a two-night minimum, you'll have fewer holes, boosting your occupancy rate and, thus, your income.

Some hosts, myself included, will allow one-night stays at times. I don't recommend doing this on a regular basis or when you're brand-new to STR ownership, as many one-night stays are for parties. Guests check in, throw a party, and leave the next day. However, if the circumstances are right, one-night stays can be lucrative and can sometimes get you to 100 percent occupancy. Stick to a two-night minimum when starting out, but if you do want to fill a few one-night holes, set a higher-than-average rate. This will tend to weed out parties. Those who are truly looking for nice accommodations when they pass through for the evening will usually have no problem paying a higher rate.

As far as maximum-night stays, check out your state laws on how long of a stay constitutes long-term tenancy and at what point guests earn tenants' rights. If they spend enough nights to have tenants' rights, you'll have to do a full eviction to remove them from your property if they refuse to leave. In my state, long-term tenancy is reached at thirty days, so it would be unwise to accept any stays longer than twenty-nine nights.

Depending on your market, don't accept any stays longer than two weeks. Around the ten-day mark, guests start asking for discounts to reward them for their long stay. If you buy in the right market, you can make more money by charging guests a higher price per night for shorter stays that add up to two weeks, rather than giving one guest a discount to stay for two weeks straight.

Age Restrictions and the Fair Housing Act

Many owners set a minimum age for guests to be allowed to rent their properties, the most common being 25. This won't guarantee that all guests will be over the age of 25 in every booking—that would be impossible to monitor—but it does give pause to those younger renters who might be looking for a party pad. While some people believe this could be construed as ageism, age is not a protected class according to the Fair Housing Act from www.hud.gov, which says:

> Title VIII of the Civil Rights Act of 1968 (Fair Housing Act), as amended, prohibits discrimination in the sale, rental, and financing of dwellings, and in other housing-related transactions, because of race, color, religion, sex, familial status, national origin, and disability.

Therefore, you are allowed to set a minimum age for renting your property. While there are certainly many responsible young adults out there, it's more a question of a few bad apples having ruined it for everyone. We'll often receive inquiries from very polite younger guests acknowledging that they are aware of our age limit, explaining the purpose of their trip to our area, and promising to be respectful of our property. Sometimes we accept them, sometimes we don't. Use your best judgment when speaking with and screening potential guests who are under 25.

Instant Booking Settings

Instant bookings are those that guests can make at the click of a button on the major platforms without having to speak with or be approved by you first. Many new investors don't allow instant bookings because they are afraid of opening their properties up to bad guests. However, it can be a very lucrative tool if you follow a few best practices:

1. Guests must have a profile photo.
2. Guests must have a government-issued ID uploaded to the platform.
3. Guests must have at least one review from other hosts.

These requirements won't weed out every single bad guest, but they will at least ensure that you're dealing with a real person who has used the platform before.

Rental Agreements

The rental agreement should set expectations for your guests and clearly define exactly what it is they are signing up for when renting your property. When putting together an STR agreement, you don't have to start from scratch. There are lots of great resources and templates online that provide a good baseline.

At a minimum, an STR agreement should specify the following:

1. Obligations and expectations of the guest
2. An outline of cancellation and refund policies
3. Pet policies
4. Occupancy rules
5. Rules about events
6. Security deposits
7. Limitation of liability
8. What will happen if either party violates the terms of the agreement

Your local attorney can draw up a rental agreement that is binding and enforceable if you ever needed to refer to it in a dispute. If you are starting with an online template, have your attorney look it over to ensure that it covers you adequately based on the differing laws of each state and market. In order for the rental agreement to be considered part of the booking on most platforms, you must mention it in your listing. You should also outline the agreement in communications with your guest on your chosen platform's messaging app.

Security Deposits

How you handle security deposits will depend on your comfort level; there is no wrong way. A very loose rule of thumb to follow is this: If the purchase price of the property is more than $500,000, the security deposit is $250. If the purchase price of the property is less than $500,000, the security deposit is $150. Each booking platform will have a different setup for security deposits.

Vrbo offers several options for charging the security deposit to the guest. For instance, you can charge them a "real" security deposit that comes out of their bank account. The money sits in an escrow account until a security claim has been filed by the host. If no such claim is filed, the deposit is either manually or automatically refunded to the guest.

Airbnb charges what some call "fake" security deposits. Airbnb is a very pro-guest platform. Its goal is to put butts in seats, so to speak. It does have a security deposit option, but the deposit does not actually get charged back to the guest. If damage occurs during a stay that was booked through Airbnb, you'll need to file a claim with the Resolution Center. At that point, the guest may or may not pay the damage resolution.

No matter how you set up security deposits for your properties, here's some timeless advice that may sound crazy but will allow you to run your business with great success: Do not file damage claims or resolutions unless the damage is severe. (I told you it was going to sound crazy!) My reasoning is simple: Hitting guests with damage resolutions equals bad reviews. In fact, damage to a small, inexpensive item is actually an opportunity to leverage a good review.

Let's say the guest breaks a lamp. The window to file a claim on a guest ends when the next guest checks in—which, in many cases, will be the same day—while the window for a guest to leave you a review is two weeks. So, unfortunately, you almost always have to entangle yourself in the damage claim situation with a guest before they have left you a review. When the guest is charged $100 for a lamp that they may or may not have broken (it's very difficult to prove), you have pretty much guaranteed yourself a bad review. In any case, it's unlikely the guest caused the damage on purpose, so a simple farewell message could be: "No worries about the lamp! Please travel safe, and thanks again!" This acknowledges that you noticed the damage but you aren't worried about it. If they did, in fact, break the lamp, this approach makes them feel obligated to leave you a positive review for being so cool about it.

The alternative—"We will be sending a $100 resolution on that twelve-year-old lamp that was in the house before we even bought it because you're a jerk and you broke it" (no matter how you word it, that's exactly how it will come across)—will result in a bad review. The guest most likely won't pay the resolution anyway. Just get a new lamp and chalk it up to the cost of doing business.

That being said, if a renter does cause significant damage to your property, call the rental platform immediately and document all of the damage with photos. Make sure that your cleaner knows to send you photos as soon as they find damage, because if the next guest checks in before the booking platform is notified of any damage and potential claims, you lose the ability to file the claim.

Discounts and When to Give Them

During your journey as an STR investor and host, you are going to be asked for discounts. There are two types of discounts that guests will ask for:

1. The up-front discount on price per night.
2. The "I'm not happy with something" discount after check-in.

Anytime a guest asks for a discount up front before even booking, the answer is no. If they're already being high-maintenance by asking you to change your prices for them, they are going to make a terrible guest when they actually check in. My only exception to this rule is for members of the military and first responders. Anyone else who asks for a discount and gets one up front is going to continue to ask for more leading up to and during their stay. Just don't do it.

The "I'm not happy with something" discount should be considered on a case-by-case basis. There will be times when there is a legitimate issue with the property and the guest should receive a discount for it. But there will also be plenty of times when a guest tries to find things wrong with the property in order to receive a discount. Let me give a few examples to better explain what I mean.

We once had a guest in one of our cabins in Tennessee. It was the middle of summer, and right around dinnertime, the HVAC unit went out. We were unable to secure an HVAC technician to fix it until the next morning, and it was so hot that the guest had to stay in a hotel. This was a situation in which a discount was warranted. We gave the guest that night for free and a little extra for the trouble they went through getting a hotel.

Conversely, every now and then a guest will call to say the hot tub isn't clean. In that case, we apologize and send our cleaner out immediately. Whether the hypothetical hot tub was or was not actually dirty, do not offer a discount if the guest doesn't ask for one. In most cases, the guest is satisfied that their issue was attended to promptly. If they do ask for a discount and the hypothetical hot tub was, in fact, dirty, give them a small discount. If the hypothetical hot tub was not dirty, let them know the issue was attended to promptly. Although it was found that the hot tub was not dirty, the housekeeper cleaned it anyway, and no discount is warranted at this time.

Most guests will forget it at that point. However, there will be some who push harder to try and take advantage. I once had a guest who noticed dirt in our hot tub. We called the housekeeper to clean it, which she did promptly. He then called to say that the new water in the hot tub was cloudy. We let him know that we run on well water and that it can be cloudy at times depending upon the mineral (iron, in this case) content in the well and the amount of rain we have had recently. He asked that the housekeeper come back out a second time to do something about the iron. He then complained about the chemicals the housekeeper used to clean the hot tub, because some random person on Reddit told him there were other, organic products that could have been used. He complained about multiple other items during his stay that no other guest had ever complained about (this property had more than a hundred five-star reviews). This is an example of a person who does not deserve a discount. Though you may be wondering, "What about the review?" We'll get to review troubleshooting in Chapter Eleven.

Cancellation Policies

Your property and market will determine the best cancellation policy for you, but it is wise to go with the strictest cancellation policy possible. If your property is in a heavily traveled vacation market, you don't want people tying up a property that could have booked six times between when that guest books and when they cancel. However, if your property is in a less heavily traveled area, you'll want to offer a more lenient policy in order to attract more bookings.

A strict cancellation policy gives you greater control. Guests won't receive automatic refunds from the platform; you'll have to issue them manually instead. On the other hand, if your policy is lenient and a guest cancels at the last minute (typically the most relaxed policy is just twenty-four hours before check-in), they will receive a refund automatically from the platform without your approval.

If you're in an STR-friendly market and you get a cancellation, you should rush to your booking platform to raise the rates on those canceled dates before the next guest has a chance to book. (By the way, if you are in a market where a cancellation means you won't be able to pay your mortgage, you're in the wrong place.) Of course, there are exceptions, such as low season, but for the most part, you should be dealing with a fairly high-volume property if you've chosen your market wisely. That's why we're here, right? The more guests we have, the more cash we make!

Cancellation Policies for Weather and Natural Disasters

There's no way to avoid severe weather and natural disasters, so it's crucial to have a strong cancellation policy in place before these situations arise. Put it right in your listing copy: "We do not give refunds due to weather or natural disasters." Why? Because you don't want guests canceling two weeks out because they saw snow in the forecast or a tropical storm that may or may not reach hurricane status.

Is that to say you shouldn't ever offer a refund if the guest needs to cancel due to a hurricane? Absolutely not. The universe will reward you for doing them a favor, especially if the situation is beyond anyone's control. You just don't want to be obligated if it's obvious the guest is using the weather forecast as an excuse to get a refund. Be sure to clearly highlight cancellation policies and procedures in the listing so that when a guest contacts you about canceling, you can simply say, "Refer to line X of the listing regarding cancellations due to weather and natural disasters."

EVICTIONS

In the event that a guest is blatantly and severely breaking the rules, you may need to kick them out. The operative word here is "severely." Don't threaten to kick guests out over one extra person, or because you saw them smoking on the porch, or because your nosy neighbor smelled weed. They need to be doing something really substantial to warrant an eviction. Examples include: throwing a big party when the listing says no parties or events; sneaking animals into a non-pet-friendly rental; conducting illegal business, such as prostitution; or refusing to check out. I have a friend whose cleaner saw her guests checking in to her property with several uncaged birds. They were loose in the house to poop on everything and claw the furniture where they perched. This is a situation that warrants eviction.

The most common reason for eviction I've heard of (but, personally, haven't dealt with) is a guest refusing to leave. If this situation arises, contact the platform on which they booked for guidance through the process for removing a guest. If you feel that you or your property are in danger and you need to take more immediate action, contact local authorities to remove the guest.

Chapter 9

SETTING UP SYSTEMS

When your business runs like clockwork, you can finally go off the clock!

—MIKE MICHALOWICZ, "CLOCKWORK"

To streamline and automate your self-management process, you'll need three core platforms or apps:

1. A channel manager
2. A pricing manager
3. A scheduling manager (sometimes these last two are built into the channel manager platform)

CHANNEL MANAGERS

Channel managers do a vast number of things to make your job as a host significantly less demanding. In a nutshell, a channel manager is a centralized system for storing and organizing bookings and communication across several channels. Below are a few of the key functions of a channel manager:

1. **Listing syncing.** A channel manager brings together your listings across all booking platforms and OTAs into one easy-to-use dashboard.

2. **One-time content uploading.** This allows you to make edits to your listing directly in the dashboard. The channel manager will then distribute those edits to all the channels where your listing is posted online. This way, you don't have to make changes to each individual platform.

3. **Cross-channel calendar syncing.** When a guest books on one platform, the channel manager software automatically blocks off those dates on all other platforms.

4. **One in-box.** All communications across all platforms are pulled into one unified in-box, so you can respond to guests on any platform from one place.

5. **Autoresponder and messaging templates.** These are invaluable tools. Most of the major booking platforms' algorithms will place you higher or lower on the property search list based on how quickly you respond to inquiries. Autoresponders are an easy way to make sure your responses go out instantaneously and to answer any FAQs. We utilize auto-messaging templates for the following:

   - **Check-in instructions.** These automatically go out to guests twenty-four hours before check-in. They include the exact address of the property (never give that out more than twenty-four hours prior to check-in), directions, door code, and any other major information guests will need to know before checking in.

   - **Halfway-point check-in.** We have our channel manager set to check in with guests halfway through their stay just to say hello and make sure that everything is going well. Most of the time, they respond with something like, "Great, thanks." It makes them feel like the hosts care about them and want them to have a great stay.

   - **Check-out instructions.** Our channel manager automatically sends instructions twenty-four hours before checkout, detailing the way everything needs to be left at the end of the stay.

A few of the most popular channel managers among STR investors are:

1. YourPorter
2. iGMS
3. Guesty
4. Hostfully
5. Syncbnb

PRICING MANAGERS

Setting your prices can be confusing initially. When you first post your listing, you will have to price your nights manually, since you'll have no reviews. Take a look at neighboring properties and undercut them a little in order to start filling your calendar. Once you are steadily booked, it is time to move to an automated pricing manager.

A pricing manager is a tool that pulls pricing data from other similar properties in your market and dynamically prices your property accordingly. These tools will optimize your price per night based on a number of factors, including seasonality, day of the week, local special events, competitor availability, and how far out the booking date is. Some channel managers (usually the more expensive ones) have pricing managers built into their systems, but there are several stand-alone pricing management tools available that will sync with most channel managers on the market. Some of the most popular are:

1. Beyond Pricing
2. Wheelhouse
3. PriceLab

Do *not* use Airbnb's built-in pricing tool. Airbnb's goal is not to optimize booking prices and revenue for hosts, but to offer affordable prices to its guests. Instead, pay a little extra for a tool that is designed to benefit you financially as an investor rather than to provide the cheapest accommodations for guests.

SCHEDULING MANAGERS

I used to spend an hour each month going through all my calendars and making a list of turn dates for my cleaners. Not only was this stressful, but I had to watch the calendar like a hawk for any last-minute bookings throughout the month and update my cleaners accordingly.

Luckily, there are a number of housekeeper scheduling automation apps that are compatible with most of the major channel managers. They work something like this: When a guest books, a notification is sent to your housekeeper, alerting them that they need to clean on a certain date. The housekeeper then acknowledges the cleaning on their end, and the owner receives a notification that the cleaning is on the house-keeper's schedule. Currently, the two major scheduling managers are TurnoverBnB and Automatebnb.

Alternatively, your channel management software might have the capability to export dates and calendars to Google or iCal. In that case, you can invite your housekeeper to access the calendar. The channel manager will automatically update the calendar as bookings come in, and your cleaner will always have an updated schedule at their fingertips.

What if your cleaner doesn't have a smartphone or a computer? No problem. My housekeeper didn't have a true computer at first. Instead, she worked primarily off an older cell phone. For a minimal investment of $200, we bought her a Chromebook laptop, created a Gmail account for her, and set up all the calendar syncing before mailing it to her. Now she has a dedicated work computer that she can take with her anywhere to view her cleaning calendar at any time.

OTHER USEFUL TOOLS

Automated Sales and Occupancy Tax Remittance Platform
All bookings on the major platforms will have an associated state sales tax and, in most cases, a local occupancy tax as well. Depending on the market, the different booking platforms will have different setups for paying sales tax. On some platforms, it will be up to the host to collect and remit state sales and local occupancy taxes. On others, the platform will collect and remit the sales tax on the booking, while the host collects and remits the local occupancy tax. This can get confusing rather quickly, especially if you own properties in multiple markets across multiple states. Contact your local codes or tax office to ensure that you are remitting your taxes correctly.

You can automate sales and occupancy tax remittance with a platform called Avalara MyLodgeTax. This platform is compatible with most of the major booking platforms and keeps you and your listings in compliance. MyLodgeTax will review your local tax obligations. All you have to do is report your earnings to the app each tax period, and it will automatically withdraw the taxes from your designated account and remit them on your behalf.

Smart Home Tools

Smart home tools can be a great asset to any STR investor, as they let you control certain aspects of your property over Wi-Fi. Standard smart home tools include:

1. **Wi-Fi smart lock.** There are dozens of Wi-Fi-compatible door locks on the market, and while they are a bit more expensive than a non-Wi-Fi digital keypad, they will make your life much easier. If a guest forgets to lock the door when they check out, you can lock it remotely. If a code doesn't work, you can change it remotely.

   Do not use a coded lockbox with a key inside as the primary, or only, access for guests. You don't want to deal with guests losing keys. However, in the event that a lock runs out of batteries or there is some other technological glitch, best practice is to have a backup lockbox or two hidden somewhere around the property with keys inside.

   I once had a guest who, after a few cocktails, could not manage to enter the key code on the door correctly. She made so many attempts that the lock ran out of batteries. This was a situation where having a hidden but easily accessible lockbox with keys inside came in handy.

2. **Smart thermostat.** Smart thermostats connect to Wi-Fi and can be controlled remotely from a smartphone app. They can be really useful for managing the temperature between guests, and they can also help identify HVAC issues. If you have the thermostat set to a certain temperature but the room does not reach the set temperature, it may be time to call an HVAC technician to check things out before a guest makes a complaint.

3. **Exterior cameras.** Cameras can be a really amazing tool for STR hosts. They give you the ability to see things like illegal parking, document whether the trash has been taken out, catch parties before they happen, and more. However, cameras can also be a very bad thing for STR hosts and, if misused, can lead to bad reviews. It all depends on your ability to roll with the punches.

I had a client a few years ago who would watch her cameras obsessively. If a guest went outside to smoke, had one extra person in their group who was not accounted for on the booking, or was grilling too close to the house, she would yell at the guest through the camera. Of course, each guest she did this to felt like their privacy had been violated and, naturally, mentioned that in their public review of the property. My client cost herself a lot of good reviews and, ultimately, cash flow by behaving this way.

In most cases, that one extra person is not going to single-handedly burn the house down, the guy taking a smoke break in the driveway is not going to chain-smoke a case of Marlboros on your couch, and guests need to be allowed to just grill some burgers. Your guests are on vacation, so let them vacation. If watching your cameras is going to cause you too much anxiety, don't have them. However, if you can be reasonable and utilize your cameras only to ensure the property is running smoothly, they're a great thing to have. In my experience, video doorbells and floodlight camera systems are the most popular and easiest to use.

4. **Noise sensors.** In some markets, noise is a big issue that can cause you to lose your STR permit with just a few complaints. Sensors, such as NoiseAware, can be installed around the home to monitor noise levels. They connect to Wi-Fi and will send you a notification as soon as the noise reaches your preset limit. This way, you have the opportunity to get ahead of any noise complaints from your neighbors.

While these tools can be a boon to any remote self-manager, they can present certain complications for guests. Before installing any smart home devices in your STR, make sure that you are familiar with them yourself. You'll need to leave clear instructions for your guests. Never assume that guests can figure out how to work something on their own. Write out instructions that a five-year-old could understand.

For example, we have a hot tub at one of our properties that goes into sleep mode if you press too many buttons. Whenever this happened, guests would send us a message and complain that the hot tub wasn't working. In reality, the guest had just put the hot tub to sleep. A quick printout and posting of the instructions on how to operate the hot tub took care of that problem.

FURNISHING AN STR

Depending on the market you're in, STRs may not come fully furnished. In that case, you'll need to choose a theme and a color scheme that are in line with the market. Palm Springs house? Midcentury modern furniture and bright colors are great. Austin townhome? Go with clean simplicity. If you furnish a beach house like a cabin in the mountains, it's going to feel weird and disconnected. Stick to the market aesthetic.

In terms of the furniture itself, do not pinch pennies. Goodwill and hand-me-down items that don't match or are a bit worn will work against you. At the same time, you don't want to go for the most expensive and impressive furniture either, because it will get worn out quickly. Go for new, durable, mid-priced pieces. You want the furniture to be able to withstand the wear and tear of short-term guests yet be easily replaceable if needed.

Here's how to furnish each room so that it has everything a renter needs to feel at home.

1. **Living room:** Ample seating by way of a comfortable couch-and-loveseat combo or armchairs, a coffee table, some sort of media cabinet under the television, and side tables.
2. **Bedrooms:** A sturdy and comfortable bed, side tables, a dresser, and a full-length mirror.
3. **Kitchen:** Pots and pans, a cookie sheet, spatulas and cooking spoons, a knife block, a cutting board, a Crock-Pot or Instant Pot, a coffee maker (or better, use a Keurig/drip combo so that guests can choose whether to make a single cup or a full pot), plates and bowls, coffee mugs, drinking glasses, wine glasses, a pizza roller, and a set of eating utensils.

When decorating your STR, keep it simple. The property needs to feel like a vacation accommodation, so don't add a bunch of knickknacks or photos of yourself and your family. It's uncomfortable for guests to feel like they're staying in someone's house while the owner is away. A few pieces of wall art in each room and minimalist decorations will look the sharpest in photos.

SETUP AND STOCKING

In addition to the basics, an STR should have all the creature comforts of a home, not just a small assortment of gadgets and utensils that put it one notch above a hotel.

Entertainment

A comfortable STR should include a television in the common areas and one in each bedroom. While older guests will prefer standard cable, younger guests will prefer streaming. You will likely need to set up a combination of both, such as standard cable and streaming services in the living room and game room, and streaming services in all the bedrooms. Installing cable boxes in each bedroom can get expensive but can be beneficial, especially in vacation markets that attract a lot of elderly guests who may not be familiar with streaming services.

Always choose the fastest internet option available in the area. Not only will this improve the performance of streaming services, but it will be a big plus for any travelers who work remotely during their stay.

Sheets and Towels

STRs need at least three sets of sheets and towels: one set of sheets on the bed and one set of towels in the bathroom, one of each set in the laundry room, and one backup set in the owner's closet. It will save your cleaner time if there's a last-minute booking, and it will help in case guests spill anything on the linens. It's also a good idea to have a few quilts or throw blankets accessible to guests in an unlocked closet to use as needed.

Towel count will depend on the number of bathrooms in the property. My rule of thumb is four towels, two hand towels, and four washcloths per bathroom. You'll also want to provide either individually packaged makeup-remover wipes or black washcloths with the word "makeup" embroidered on them. Towel color can be market-specific and will largely depend on your housekeeper's preference. Bright white is preferred in most markets so that they can be bleached; however, some housekeepers prefer khaki or light gray to hide any stains or dinginess. Always ask your housekeeper which color is standard and preferred before buying!

Some cleaners will offer to automatically reorder sheets and towels for you when they start to wear out. Those who offer this service for an extra fee will usually provide whatever is cheapest. Ask your housekeeper to let you know when the sheets or towels need to be replaced, that way you can order a few more sets online and stay in control of the quality of sheets and towels provided. Nice sheets and towels do make a difference in guest comfort, so this is not an area where it pays to pinch pennies.

Paper Products

You'll need to stock toilet paper and paper towels as well. As with sheets and towels, some housekeepers will offer to keep these products stocked for you for an extra fee per cleaning. Again, try to stay in control of the products being used by setting up an automatic shipment from online retailers to be delivered directly to your housekeeper's home or warehouse.

How much of each item should you leave out for guests? Leaving too much can cut into your cash flow, so keep a max of two rolls of toilet paper per bathroom and two rolls of paper towels in the kitchen. Make it clear to guests in the FAQ or welcome section of your listing how many of each item will be left out for them. We explain that we provide a "starter kit" of paper products but that guests who plan to stay for longer than two or three days will most likely need to supply their own once the starter kit runs out.

Miscellaneous Kitchen and Cleaning Items

When it comes to disposable kitchen items, options abound. Below is a short list of items you should stock and a few you don't have to bother with.

1. **Spices.** Most guests will not remember to purchase spices when they make their beginning-of-vacation trip to the grocery store. Buy a pre-stocked spice rack with all the basics, and guests will always be set. The good thing about spices is it takes a long time for them to run out, so this will be a biannual expense at most.

2. **Ground coffee and filters.** Whether you offer a drip coffee maker or a Keurig is up to you, but either way, you'll want to supply single-use packets of creamer and sweetener for guests. If you have a drip maker, provide ground coffee and filters. The best way to keep coffee stocked is to buy a few extra-large canisters and a large, clear decorative jar. Keep the decorative jar by the coffeepot and the ground coffee in the owner's closet. Have the cleaner refill the clear jar with coffee before new guests arrive. This way, guests can see that coffee is provided, and they don't have to feel like they are sharing a can of coffee with every guest who has stayed at your place before them.

Insofar as supplying K-Cups, that is up to each owner. Some owners provide a K-Cup carousel that the cleaners refill with different coffees and teas for guests. However, K-Cups are pretty expensive to keep stocked. A BYO K-Cups policy is totally acceptable and not out of the ordinary.

3. **Cooking spray.** Guests often forget this grocery item. Buy a case of cooking spray for the owner's closet and have the cleaner restock as needed.

4. **Dishwasher and laundry detergent.** These items also fall under the "starter kit" category. Do not leave your guests full boxes or jugs of detergent. It's messy and often ends up disappearing when guests check out. Instead, get a few clear decorative containers to store dish pods by the kitchen sink and laundry pods by the washer/dryer.

5. **Cleaning supplies.** Guests will need to be able to clean up after themselves during their stay. Make sure they have access to a broom, mop, or wet Swiffer and a multi-surface cleaning spray at a minimum. Also leave a few trash bags (not an entire roll) for guests to use when the trash cans get full.

Specialty Items

Many STR investors get caught up in wanting to make their place "special" or "an experience." That's totally fine. It's great to be invested in making sure your guests enjoy their time at your property, which is paramount to good reviews. However, some ideas are better left alone. I'm often asked if I leave gift baskets or bottles of wine for guests. The answer is a resounding no. You've likely seen this practice on an HGTV show or two, but there are a number of reasons you shouldn't do it.

First and foremost, leaving alcohol for guests is a bad idea. I have a client who recently closed on a mountain property with my team. On the first night of his very first booking, one of his guests drunkenly fell off the second-floor deck and had to be extracted from the side of the hill by the fire department. The guest suffered only a few bumps and bruises and ultimately found the entire situation to be nothing more than a hilarious story to tell his drinking buddies. But think about what could have happened if the guest had been seriously injured or had not been good-natured about the incident. What if the host had left a bottle of wine for the guests, and they decided to blame the host for encouraging the drinking by supplying alcohol? It's best to let the guests be in charge of their own alcohol consumption.

We tried leaving gift baskets in our first few STRs, and this is what we learned:

1. Guests don't care.
2. They are not going to thank you.
3. They will forget all about your gift basket if something doesn't go right or if they find a speck of dirt.

Leaving food products in gift baskets also invites allergy issues. A friend of mine with an STR in Texas left gift baskets for all her guests with assorted snacks. Once, the child of a guest ate a peanut butter granola bar from the gift basket. The child had a peanut allergy and experienced an allergic reaction. Guess who the mother blamed for this incident? The owner.

Besides, gift baskets don't produce any sort of value for you as the investor as far as guest appreciation is concerned, so in my opinion, they aren't worth the time and effort. Simply leave a nice note on the first page of a guest book for your guests instead.

Bedbugs

I hate to be the one to break it to you, but if you own STRs, bedbugs are not a question of *if* but *when*. However, if you are diligent in your preventive measures, your downtime will be minimal. Here are a few relatively inexpensive ways to prevent bedbugs:

1. Use mattress (and box spring, if you have them) encasements. Bedbug encasements are not to be confused with mattress protectors. Mattress protectors fit over the mattress like a fitted sheet. Encasements zip the entire mattress inside of them. This zippered function prevents bedbugs from coming into contact with, and making their home in, the actual mattress. Encasements can be found at any big-box store or online for less than $50 per bed.
2. Pay for professional monthly interior and exterior pest control that includes bedbug checks and prevention.
3. Do not require your guests to strip the beds for checkout. Although many STR owners do so, the problem is that the sheets will be crumpled into a ball and difficult to inspect. If the sheets are left on the bed, the housekeeper can easily check for the tiny black or dark brown blood spots that bedbugs leave behind. Ask your housekeeper

to take a quick look for evidence of bedbugs before stripping the sheets.

Pack 'n Plays

Whether to provide a pack 'n play for guests with babies and toddlers is a topic of contention among STR hosts. Many gurus preach the value of providing a pack 'n play, and as the mother of two children under two years old, I wholeheartedly agree that it's a huge pain to bring your own on every trip.

On the other hand, pack 'n plays can break or wear out over time. The possibility of providing a pack 'n play that malfunctions or isn't set up properly makes me break into a cold sweat. Instead, provide guests with the website of a local retailer that rents pack 'n plays to travelers.

Chapter 10

LAUNCHING YOUR LISTING

When you really want something, the whole universe conspires to help you achieve it.

—PAULO COELHO, "THE ALCHEMIST"

Once you've set up and stocked your property, acquired great listing photos, and written amazing listing copy, it's time to go live! While going live sounds like a mere press of a button, it's quite a bit more involved than that.

You'll need to start building your listing once you get through the appraisal contingency on your transaction (assuming that you are buying a turnkey property). Many investors get around this by posting their listing as soon as possible and blocking off a bunch of dates because the property is not yet ready to be rented. This will make it difficult to get your first few bookings. On most major booking platforms, when a new listing is posted, the platform will drive more traffic to that listing than to other listings in order to help get it up and running. When you post a listing as live but have a bunch of dates blocked off, this tells the algorithm on the platform that the listing is unavailable. You therefore won't get that initial SEO boost. For larger properties, you should go live ten days before you're ready for your first guest. For smaller properties, go live maybe five to seven days early. Never post a listing more than fourteen days before you are ready for your first guest check-in.

Before you go live, plan a little orientation time for yourself. Set aside an hour to go through and familiarize yourself with all the different booking apps (and the channel management platform you've chosen). Once you feel comfortable with the platforms and all the settings are calibrated how you want them, you're ready!

THE $4,000-A-NIGHT METHOD

One issue many hosts run into is the inability to add or change a couple of important settings in the listing until it is actually live and available to be booked. For example, you won't be able to connect your channel manager and other automation tools. Connecting and syncing automation tools can take up to an hour to do correctly, and you don't want bookings coming in before they're set up. You also cannot add your cleaning fee and a few other important items until the listing is live. So to deter bookings before you're ready, set your base rate at $4,000 per night. Assuming you have not purchased a $20 million mansion, this rate should be so high that no guest would possibly book your STR. (And if you did, in fact, buy a $20 million mansion, set the rate for $40,000 per night.) The point is to make the price so high that no one will book it during the time it takes you to get the rest of your listing set up. Make sure that the smart pricing option is turned off.

DISCOUNTS AND HOLIDAYS

When you do go live, the major booking platforms are going to prompt you to offer a 20 percent discount for your first few bookings in order for your listing to get some traction. Before you do this, go into your calendar and ensure that your three-day weekend and holiday rates are very high. The last thing you need is for your Christmas or Labor Day dates to get booked at a steep discount. The holidays are going to get booked at a high rate regardless, so there is no point in giving them away. Instead, offer the discount for dates that are harder to book.

CHECK-IN AND CHECKOUT TIMES

Guests can be particular about check-in and checkout times, especially when flying with large pieces of luggage they need to store. Therefore, before the listing goes live, make sure they are correct, especially in high-volume markets. If you neglect to include these times in your listing and wind up with a checkout and a check-in at the same time on the same day, you might have a problem on your hands.

INSTANT BOOKING

Make sure that the instant book function is turned off when you first go live. You are going to get hit with bookings pretty quickly, and with a brand-new property, you'll need to vet those guests a little more thoroughly. Once you have been live for a few days and have a number of good bookings, or your calendar is full for about a month out, you can turn on the instant book feature. Many channel management platforms require that the instant book feature be enabled in order to work properly.

PAYMENT OPTIONS

Some of the major booking platforms do not have options when it comes to payments. On these platforms, you will usually get a direct deposit into your account the date of check-in. On other platforms, however, you can choose either a one-time payment or a payment broken up into two or three installments. If you allow your guests to pay in installments, it is your responsibility to make sure they pay the second and third installments. The platform will allow them to get to check-in day without having paid in full.

Since our properties are in high-volume markets, we don't allow guests to pay in installments. We don't have the time to chase down second and third payments or deal with guests making excuses for why they can't pay. Additionally, if the guest makes payments long before the check-in date and then they need to cancel, it's up to the owner to issue them a refund. It can be tough to have the money in your account before the guest checks in, as it artificially inflates the amount of cash in the account.

I once represented a buyer in a transaction where the STR property allowed three payment installments. The seller insisted that we do a ninety-day close to accommodate future bookings. My buyer didn't want to do that, so we offered all kinds of solutions in order to arrive at a thirty-day close without canceling any of the guests' vacations. Finally, the seller came clean, admitting that he had already spent the first installments from the future bookings and did not have the money to refund his guests so they could rebook with my client. This ended up killing the deal. If you're savvy enough to be reading this book, then I don't think I have to expand further on why it's not a great idea to spend money you haven't made yet.

Finally, when you do go live, make sure that you are in front of a computer and have some time carved out to troubleshoot and field any incoming bookings. Do not go live right before walking into an important meeting. There are going to be some things you'll need to adjust once your listing is live. Give yourself at least an hour to make any necessary adjustments and answer the first few inquiries.

Chapter 11

MANAGING YOUR RENTAL

"Is it hard?"

"Not if you have the right attitudes. It's having the right attitudes that's hard."

—ROBERT M. PIRSIG, *ZEN AND THE ART OF MOTORCYCLE MAINTENANCE*

There are a few things every host goes through when they're new to managing their STR properties. Learn from these common experiences so you can maximize your cash flow—even in the first few months of management.

BOOKINGS ARE SLOW TO START

If getting bookings is taking longer than expected, the culprit is probably your listing—most likely the photos. I recently had an investor send me a link to his listing because it hadn't received any bookings. The property is in a high-volume market in a great location, so the lack of bookings didn't make sense. When I took a look, the issue was definitely the photos. Although the property was less than a hundred yards from one of the most beautiful beaches in North America, the primary photo was of the sign in front of the condo community. Inside, there was very little furniture and decor. The walls, carpet, and kitchen tile were khaki, and the couch was off-white leather. The property looked like a giant monochrome box.

I suggested that he change the profile photo to an aerial shot of the property with an arrow pointing to the beach, and brighten things up with colorful rugs and artwork on the walls. Once he made those few adjustments, the property started booking almost immediately.

If your listing is slow to get bookings at the beginning, take a look at what you can improve. It's rarely the case that the property was a bad choice. Usually it's just that the presentation needs to be enhanced.

Also, when posting a new listing, include something like "new owner special" in the headline. As potential guests peruse the booking platform, they may be wary of a listing that looks nice but has no reviews. They might think it's a scam or a fake listing, or that there's something wrong with the property. Having "new owner special" in the headline will explain why there are no reviews and why your property may be cheaper than other comparable listings.

GREEN LIGHT SYNDROME

Once the bookings start rolling in, you're going to feel great. You'll feel accomplished, like you made the best decision ever, like you just invented fire and opened the door to an entire new world of income—all of which will be true. As that bank account starts growing, you're going to want to take over the world with STRs. You'll want to get all your friends involved, and, mark my words, you'll want to start an STR management business or write a course for people to buy online. I call this green light syndrome.

Every single investor goes through a period at the beginning of their STR investment career when they are on cloud nine and all-in on STRs. This usually happens during the first month of their first listing going live. They think, "Oh my God, I'm making money! I'm going to quit my job and manage everyone's STRs for them." Or "I'm going to create an online course that teaches people how to manage STRs! I'm going to be a guru!" I often see investors who I have recently helped acquire a property make their rounds on the STR investor Facebook groups offering management or cohosting services, or announcing their new $1,000 online course to everyone when they haven't even received their first review yet.

At the risk of bursting your bubble, I'd like to point out that thousands of people have done this. While it's incredibly exciting to get financial validation that you've made a good investment, keep calm, continue learning, and start building a down payment for your next investment. Managing other people's properties is not going to get you to financial independence faster; leveraging your W-2 income and building the down payment for your next investment will. So don't get caught up in the green lights—continue learning and stay the course. Build wealth for yourself through your own investments. Don't create a job for yourself by working on other people's investments.

GUEST INTERACTION

Guest interaction is a critical piece of the STR investing puzzle. How you interact with guests will determine your success rate. You have to balance being friendly and inviting with being a nonperson—a computer or answering service on the other end of the line. If you get too friendly with guests, they will expect too much, but if you aren't friendly enough, they will not feel taken care of.

Guest Communication

It's very important to keep all communication with your guests in the booking platform's messenger app. Do not allow them to send you texts or call you. This way, if any situation arises that requires the booking platform's involvement, all communication is documented and viewable in the platform messaging system. If some sort of miscommunication occurs in a text message or on a phone call, it becomes a "he said, she said" situation, and the platform will most likely side with the guest on any dispute. Additionally, all platforms monitor conversations to make sure hosts aren't directing guests to book off-platform. Asking potential guests to book directly with you to avoid fees is the fastest way to get kicked off the major platforms, with all your future bookings deleted. Unless you get a ton of traffic to your listing's independent website, it's not worth getting kicked off the major platforms for a direct booking here and there. Follow the rules and keep all communication on-platform.

General Guest Questions

In order to minimize time spent answering the same questions over and over again, make sure FAQs are clearly displayed in the listing. When guests ask questions, politely direct them to the section of your listing where they are answered. If you get in the habit of answering every question every time, you're letting your guest, or your business, run you rather than the other way around. Of course, if a guest has a question that's not answered in your listing, don't leave them hanging!

Setting Business Hours

A lot of hosts get caught up in feeling they need to respond to every guest immediately, all the time. While the search algorithms on the major booking platforms do reward hosts who respond immediately, this function is restricted to just the first message. As long as you respond quickly to the first message from a potential guest, your search rankings will not be affected by subsequent response times. You can set your channel manager to respond for you.

Going even one step further: Set up business hours. Whether it be for religious reasons, full-time job commitments, or just running your business like a business, you can still be highly successful with your STR without being available 24/7. There is no reason that you need to be answering messages from guests in the middle of the night. Many potential investors will ask, "But what if there is an emergency in the middle of the night and a guest needs to reach me?" If there is an emergency, the guest can contact the local authorities. If they have burned down your house, it will still be burned down when you wake up, and you can deal with it then. Time management is of the utmost importance as you grow your business, and setting business hours and boundaries early will lay a great foundation for developing successful time blocking and systems as you grow. Just make sure to clearly state your business hours in your listing and your initial communication with guests.

As you communicate with guests, remember that you are not a travel agent. While it is your job to give great customer service, make sure that all their questions are answered, and provide activity suggestions in your listing, it's not your job to host them as you would a close friend or family member. Ensure that they have everything they need for their stay, but don't feel obligated to order them extra items, book them activity passes, or provide them with any additional services. Sometimes a guest lets us know ahead of time that they will be proposing during their stay, and we'll do what we can to help. But when a guest asks us to rent them a pack 'n play, book their dog at a boarding place, or set them up with tickets to a local dinner show, we politely decline and point them in the direction of where they can handle these tasks themselves.

Message Templates

Using your channel manager, you can set up message templates. Here are a several core messages that you should set up in order to minimize guest questions:

- **The "thank you for booking" template.** This message will go out to guests as soon as they book your property. It will include a few lines thanking them for booking and conveying how excited you are that they have chosen your property for their vacation. It will also set the expectation for the communication for the rest of their trip. It will lay out when they can expect another message that will include the address and check-in instructions, as well as a few lines answering any FAQs that come up in your market prior to booking.

  For example, in my beach market, guests often ask whether they need to bring a beach wagon or bicycles. In my mountain market, they ask whether they'll need a vehicle with four-wheel drive. It might take a few bookings for you to get a feel for what the market FAQs are, but once you do, make sure they are all addressed in your "thank you for booking" message template.

- **The "check-in" template.** This message will be auto-sent by your channel manager within forty-eight hours of check-in. It will include the address of your property, directions (you'd be surprised by how many people have trouble using their GPS), door codes, Wi-Fi networks and passwords, and so on.

  Never give a guest the exact address of your property until twenty-four to forty-eight hours before check-in. They can get a very good idea of the location of the property from the maps on Airbnb and Vrbo. Giving anyone the address of an STR too far in advance leaves your property vulnerable to potential break-ins. When a guest is pushy about receiving the exact address before the forty-eight hour window, this can be an indication of a scam, and it may be wise to ask them to cancel and find other accommodations if they are unhappy with your address policies.

This check-in message will also reiterate your house rules, distances to major attractions, and restaurant recommendations. Don't forget to repeat the check-in time. Guests will often ask to check in early, so be sure to add a line stating that early check-ins are not allowed. You may not think that allowing an early check-in is a big deal, but it has the potential to create a lot of headaches for you. For example, if you have a checkout at 11 a.m. and a check-in at 3 p.m., your housekeeper will need an adequate amount of time to clean between guests. Allowing early check-in puts extra pressure on your housekeeper, and things might be missed. Plus, if you manage multiple properties, it can become difficult to keep up with differing check-in policies. Best practice is to just stick to a no-early-check-in policy and explain to guests that this ensures the housekeeper has enough time to get the property in tip-top shape for their arrival.

Another tip: Place the door code three-fourths of the way down in your check-in message copy. This forces the guest to read all the other rules before they find the door code. If you put it right at the top or at the very bottom, they are less likely to read the rest of the message with important information about the property, which could result in annoying, redundant messages from guests during their stay.

- **The "checkout" template.** Schedule this message, which includes checkout instructions, to auto-send to guests twenty-four hours before checkout. In my markets, it is standard for guests to gather and dispose of all trash in the outside trash cans, put all dishes into the dishwasher and run it, and remove any food or beverages they brought with them from the refrigerator/freezer. This template also includes the checkout time. The same rule that applies for early check-ins should also apply for late checkouts. The housekeeper must have enough time to clean for the next guests.

- **Bonus template.** We use a fourth "bonus" template that auto-sends to the guest halfway through their stay. Our bonus template says something like, "Hey there, it's Luc and Avery. Hope you are enjoying your stay! How is everything? Make sure to check out our favorite activity, X!" That way, the guests feels looked after, and they don't generally ask for anything or make any complaints. They just appreciate the hospitality.

Declining a Guest

When a potential guest finds your listing on the major booking platforms and inquires about the property, you will be given four options:

1. **Accept.** Choosing this option will accept the booking and confirm the guest to stay at your property.
2. **Preapprove.** This button gives the host a chance to review the guest's questions before allowing them to book. Once you hit the preapprove button, the platform gives the guest the green light to book.
3. **Special offer.** This button allows you to change the price of the booking to something different from the quoted amount. This is usually used for discounts or adding and subtracting days from the booking.
4. **Decline.** This blocks the guest from being able to book the property. Declining a guest, while frowned upon by the platforms, is not nearly as bad as canceling someone who has already been confirmed. Use the decline button sparingly. We will talk more about how to avoid having to use the decline button in a few pages.

Many owners get so caught up in having a full rental calendar that they take on a lot of bad bookings. The quality of bookings is much more important than the quantity. You need to trim your small pumpkins off the vine so that you can pay more attention to your large pumpkins. (A fantastic book on this subject is *The Pumpkin Plan: A Simple Strategy to Grow a Remarkable Business in Any Field* by Mike Michalowicz.) The best way to avoid negative reviews is to stop potentially bad guests before they even have the opportunity to book the property. You'd be surprised how many people will give themselves away as a bad guest before their booking has even been accepted. Below are just a few examples of ways guests have busted themselves.

- "Your place is so beautiful! The pool will be perfect for my sister's bachelorette party photos!"
- "Do you have room in your driveway for ten dually trucks? Last year we brought so many people to this event that we did not have enough room to sleep in the cabin, so a lot of us had to sleep in our trucks."
- "What kind of laundry detergent do you use for your linens? I have sensitive skin and cannot tolerate many detergents. Can you use a

special detergent for our stay? Or if you could supply us with a brand-new set of sheets that have never been used, that would be ideal."

- "Would it be possible for us to have a conversation with your house-keeper before we book so that we can go over her checklist and cleaning routine to ensure that the cabin will be clean enough for us?"
- "Would it be possible for us to come see the property about a month before our stay so that we can decide if the property will be adequate for our vacation?"
- "Can you confirm that there will not be mosquitoes if we sit outside to drink wine on the deck?"

You get the idea. A bad guest isn't necessarily a partier; they can be someone who is very high-maintenance or impossible to please. It's always good to ask a few preliminary questions when they make an inquiry, or even if they use the instant book feature. Just send a quick message: "Hey there! Thank you for the interest in our property! What brings you to our neck of the woods next month?" Most guests will open up enough that you'll be able to gauge their quality.

To make it even easier on yourself, include all the pertinent information regarding parties and house rules in several different places in the listing. That way, the bad guests can weed themselves out. For example, you could set a three-car maximum and state that if a renter brings more guests than listed on their reservation, they may be asked to leave without a refund. If you mention multiple times in the listing that quiet time begins at 10 p.m., they'll find another place that will let them party until 3 a.m.

Scams
You will occasionally run into scammers on the major booking platforms. Spotting scam inquiries is pretty similar to spotting scam emails. The grammar will often be questionable, and the potential guest will tend to overexplain their trip. Their current job situation will be used as an excuse to communicate with you off-platform (via email or phone call), and they will commonly ask to pay off-platform with a cashier's check or money order. A few other common scams are:

1. Booking the trip as a surprise for someone else.
2. Overpaying the amount of the booking and then requesting a refund before the initial payment has cleared.

3. Booking a reservation that starts within the next twenty-four hours, staying in the property, and checking out before the host can discover that the payment is fraudulent.

To protect yourself and your investment, never communicate off-platform, accept payment off-platform, or allow bookings in which one person is planning a stay for someone else.

One other pretty big scam is when someone creates a copy listing of your property and posts it somewhere like Craigslist for rent. The scammer takes bookings and receives payments but never sends guests the address or any further information regarding the property. This type of scam is difficult to catch until a guest brings it to your attention. Then you'll need to go to wherever the fraudulent ad is posted and flag it for removal.

Troubleshooting Common Guest Issues

Unfortunately, there will be instances when you provide the cleanest, nicest, most affordable, and most accessible property for a guest, and they will still not be happy. Some people are just complainers. You will undoubtedly encounter such people at some point. It is also inevitable that a mistake or mishap within your control will occur. When it does, you'll have to be able to communicate effectively with the guest to reach a resolution in order to prevent a bad review. In the following paragraphs, we will discuss a few of the most common issues that come up with guests and how to resolve them.

1. **The property gets double booked.** Your channel manager has the ability to sync calendars across platforms, but if two guests book at the exact same time on different platforms, the channel manager will not have time to sync the calendars. The result is a double booking. This is a sticky situation. As a host, you never want to hit the cancel button, since you'll be penalized by the booking platform (more on this later). Instead, call both parties, explain the situation, and try to get one of them to cancel their booking. Being honest with the guests and communicating the issue as soon as possible is all you can do.

2. **Something goes wrong during a guest's stay.** Depending on how severe the issue is, you will have three options:
   - **Option 1:** Send a maintenance person over to resolve it immediately, and do not offer a discount.

- **Option 2:** If the issue is not easily fixable through a maintenance call, offer a discount for the inconvenience. The size of the discount will depend upon how significant the issue is. For example, if a toilet seat breaks and the guests have to use the other bathroom during their stay, a small discount should suffice.
- **Option 3:** Issue the guest a refund for their remaining nights. This option should be reserved for the most severe circumstances, such as bedbugs or a broken AC unit in the middle of summer which cannot be repaired for several days. In such cases, ask the guest to cancel the rest of their stay (remember, never hit the cancel button yourself), and issue them a refund for the remaining days. Do not, however, issue a refund for the nights they have already stayed. Never offer to discount the full trip— only the portion remaining after the maintenance issue arises.

3. **The housekeeper misses a cleaning.** The best course of action is to send the housekeeper over to the property immediately to clean. Offer a dinner or activity gift card to the guest, or remove the cleaning fee from their bill. Usually guests will be understanding about this if the housekeeper arrives at the property very quickly.

Guest Complaints

Sometimes, a guest will be unhappy and make a complaint to you. This could be about anything, from the bathroom not being clean enough to the hot tub not working to the kitchen being understocked. When guests make legitimate and reasonable complaints, listen to them. Even if you find them unreasonable, listen. Respond graciously and thank them for letting you know about the issue. If it is something that is fixable (and again, reasonable), take care of it.

For instance, we once had a guest complain that we didn't have any cookie sheets. It was a new listing, and they were our fourth or fifth booking. We realized that we had completely forgotten cookie sheets when we stocked the kitchen, so we paid our housekeeper a small fee to buy some cookie sheets and take them over to the guest. The guest felt heard and was very grateful that her complaint had not only been acknowledged but taken care of. Consequently, we got a great review from a happy guest. If a guest complains that the hot tub isn't working, we help them troubleshoot or send the cleaner over to ensure that the water level is high enough to cover the jets. (This is the number one reason why people complain that a hot tub doesn't work, by the way.) A happy guest equals a great review.

At times guests will make unreasonable requests, and you'll need to respond to those too. We once had a guest ask us to bring them more toilet paper during their stay. This is not a reasonable request, and we had to point them in the direction of the nearest store. On another occasion, we had a guest complain that we did not stock Worcestershire or soy sauce, his two favorite condiments. This is not a reasonable complaint, as it's unfair to expect us to stock every sauce and condiment under the sun. Again, we politely pointed them in the direction of the nearest store.

The bottom line is that despite your best efforts, things will go wrong with your listing. If a guest complains while they are in-house, take care of the problem if you can. If you cannot, be polite and gracious in your response, and never ever forget to thank them for their feedback.

Forgotten Items

Every now and then, a guest will forget something at your property. Have a plan in place with your housekeeper to deal with this. When I first started, a guest left her credit card on the coffee table. She messaged us to let us know that she believed she had left it behind, and asked us to mail it to her if we found it. Our housekeeper at the time did, in fact, find the card. We asked her to mail it, and she agreed.

Weeks later, I received an angry text from our housekeeper saying the guest she mailed the card to "owed her money," and she wanted me to call and get it for her. I was completely taken aback. Why in God's name did this random guest owe our housekeeper money? How did they even come in contact with each other? When I asked the housekeeper, she told me she had included a handwritten invoice for $7, asking the guest to pay for the time and gas it took to mail the card. The housekeeper was angry that the guest had never mailed her the $7.

This was a lesson for me on having a plan in place for all potential situations. I thought this housekeeper would just mail the credit card and bill me for her time. Never assume that a vendor will behave the way you expect them to, and set up a plan for forgotten guest items so you don't run into an awkward situation like I did.

There have been two occasions when guests have left a firearm in my unit. If this happens, don't freak out, and don't try to get it back to the guest yourself. The correct course of action is to call your local sheriff's office or police department and let them know that a guest has left behind a firearm. They will collect the firearm so that the guest can retrieve it from them.

REVIEWS

It's of the utmost importance that you attempt to get a review from every guest. The more good reviews you have, the higher up your listing will show in search results. The more visibility you receive, the more bookings you will bring in. How do you get a review from every guest? You ask them, of course! Don't feel shy or tacky about asking guests for a five-star review. If you don't ask, you don't get.

This message has worked well for me: "Thanks so much for staying with us. We hope to have you back again soon! We left a five-star review in your inbox, and we hope you will do the same for us!" It's important to let guests know that anything less than a five-star review is a bad review. Some guests mistakenly think that a four-star review is the equivalent of a four-star hotel, meaning it's great. Some guests have an "I don't give anything five stars" attitude. If you don't gently let them know that five stars is the only acceptable rating, they won't know to leave five. Of course, you don't get what you don't ask for, so always ask for that five-star review.

Review Responses

If you take nothing else from this section, remember this: Respond to all reviews, not just the negative ones. Kindly thank guests for the review, and invite them to come back anytime. If you can throw in a quick comment specific to their stay—such as, "Glad you enjoyed our favorite hike so much!"—the personal touch shows future guests that you care about each individual guest experience.

When you do get a less-than-five-star review, responding gives you the chance to publicly explain whatever perceived negative situation the guest experienced. The way you respond to negative reviews will shape the way future guests view you as a host. If you respond with snark, condescension, and attitude, you may lose a few bookings. If you respond with grace and explain what you did to fix the problem and how you will work to improve your property for future guests, you will turn negative reviews into positive ones. This is what I call "review language." When potential guests read your response and see that you have handled criticism with maturity and understanding, they will forget the negative review. If the reviewer has complained about something ridiculous, it can also be helpful to gently point out why their complaint is ridiculous—with maturity and understanding, of course.

Getting Bad Reviews Removed

Unfortunately, it is incredibly difficult to remove a bad review from any of the major booking platforms. The only reason a platform will remove a bad review is if it violates one of their review policies by including:

- Commentary about a person's social, political, or religious views.
- Profanity, name calling, and assumptions about a person's character or personality.
- Content that refers to circumstances entirely outside of another's control.
- Content about services not related to the platform (for example, transportation and meals).
- Commentary about past platform reservations, hosts, or guests, or commentary about the platform product that does not relate to the listing or host they are rating.

Unless a review violates these policies, you probably won't be able to get it taken down. However, I'll share a little trick that sometimes works: The booking platform's customer service representative will likely say something along the lines of, "This review does not violate any of our policies, so at this time we are unable to remove the review." When they do, ask them to please read you the list of policies. As they are reading, point out exactly which policy the review has violated and why. If you make a strong enough argument for why the review violates the policy, you may be able to get them to take it down. If that doesn't work, call back several times and try this method on different customer service reps. Sometimes all it takes is the right person. This goes for any customer service request for which you are not getting the answer you want. Keep calling back until you find a representative who is more willing to help you. It has worked for me more often than not.

Avoiding Negative Reviews by Not Taking Every Guest

Many STR investors get caught up in trying to book every single potential guest who shows interest in their property. This approach can be counterproductive. The best way to avoid the non-merit-based bad reviewer is to never accept their booking in the first place. While none of us have a crystal ball, you can generally tell before a guest checks in if they are going to leave a bad review. Are they asking tons of questions that are very clearly answered in the listing? Are they already requesting special treatment, favors, and rule bending?

If they are high-maintenance right off the bat, they are only going to get worse during their stay. When they do make these types of requests, politely answer in a way you know won't be pleasing to them. For example, if they ask whether you can use a specific kind of laundry detergent on all sheets and towels before their stay because they have sensitive skin, let them know that is not possible, and ask them to cancel for a full refund if that is not acceptable to them. Nine times out of ten they will cancel, and you will have avoided what was sure to be a negative review. It might feel a bit uncomfortable to turn away a guest and the potential booking income, but it will be far less painful than the three-star review dragging down your rating and hurting your search result placement.

You Can't Please Everyone

About 95 percent of the time, everything with your property will run smoothly and you'll receive great reviews from guests; 4.9 percent of the time, something will go wrong, you'll do your best to troubleshoot and keep the guests happy, and they may or may not mention it in their review. Then there's that 0.1 percent of the time when everything will go smoothly and you will still get a bad review. This review will not reflect your customer service or the quality of your property. You can't please everyone and, eventually, you will run into a guest for whom nothing is good enough.

I've had a few of these guests in my properties over the years, but one of them truly takes the cake. We own a two-bedroom cabin in the Great Smoky Mountains in a little neighborhood about five miles outside Pigeon Forge. The roads are gently rolling (not steep), wide, and nicely paved. The cabin has a view of Bluff Mountain, with big cathedral windows so that the view can be taken in from both floors. While it is definitely in a cabin community, it's on a one-acre lot and has enough trees on each side so that it feels private. The cabin offers the best of both worlds as far as proximity and privacy are concerned.

We had a guest check in for the weekend a couple of years ago. He complained about the roads immediately upon check-in and asked about any critters he might see during his stay. We told him that there are deer, foxes, raccoons, and the occasional bear. We didn't hear much from him during his stay, but when we got the notification that he had left a review, we were shocked. This individual left us a two-star review. We had no negative interaction with him, and nothing broke or malfunctioned during his stay. He even left five stars in the "cleanliness" section. Still, when we read the text of his review, it was very difficult not to laugh. The following has been edited for profanity but not grammar:

Bad Experience (2/5 stars) Stayed July 2019
I had a bad experience. The owner is a jerk I had and misunderstands whatever you ask. He is also insensitive to any issues you might have. As you know not living in the North and not being used to bears I am naturally afraid of them. This owner told me I have irrational fear. The walls on the first floor are glass which are easily broken in by a bear or a human who might want to break in. It is extremely dark at night and you are practically in a cul-de-sac by the time the police they get there should anything happen your chances of survival are slim... The trees surrounding the cabin in one part are overtaking and squirrels and other animals, climb onto the roof and walk at night over it and keep you from sleeping. I left my vacation early for personal reasons I did not request any money back and the owner was complete jerk about my personal reasons for leaving, he asked if it was because of being afraid of bears. Which is natural if you do not live within them all the time. Bears wasn't the reason I left. Overall we enjoyed our wonder time in general area its a fantastic place for tourism you are better renting off a hotel room in the heart of Gatlinburg where you can walk to the major attractions in some cases without the fear of bears.

We had offered this person a great stay, a clean property, and great service. He decided to leave a two-star review based on the hypothetical situation that a bear would stop at our property, walk up to the porch, look in the window, decide to jump through the glass, and murder each guest one by one on a whim—a situation that would likely never happen, and most certainly did not happen during his stay.

If you own vacation rentals long enough, you will meet a person like this. Take it with a grain of salt and understand that as future guests are reading your reviews, they will be able to tell the difference between a legitimate bad review and a preposterous situation like this.

GETTING UPSTREAM OF PROBLEMS

In his book *Upstream: The Quest to Solve Problems Before They Happen*, Dan Heath says, "The postmortem for a problem can be the preamble to a solution." In order to effectively solve problems with your STR, you need to create solutions so that they never occur in the first place. If a particular issue comes up in your STR more than twice, it's your fault. Take the hot tub at one of my properties that goes into sleep mode if too many buttons are pushed. After three separate guests messaged to tell us the hot tub didn't work, it became apparent that this was not the guests' fault; it was our fault for not getting upstream of the problem. In this case, we simply needed to post instructions on how to operate the hot tub. The same is true for any issue that may arise with your STR.

SCHEDULING MAINTENANCE AROUND GUESTS

Every property is going to require maintenance at some point. The most cost-efficient way to plan repairs is a method I call "letting the renters pay for it." Rather than making minor to moderate repairs up front using cash out of your own pocket, get the property up and running. This way, the property can start making money immediately. In a few months, when the off-season rolls around, you can pay for the repairs using other people's money, that is, money the property has earned from previous rentals. I've been waiting three years to make a few upgrades to two of my properties. They have been so consistently rented that I have not wanted to cut into my income to block off the calendar and make the upgrades.

In terms of general ongoing maintenance items, your housekeeper will be your eyes and ears, as they will be at the property every week. They can let you know if anything is exhibiting signs of wear and tear, if any toilets are loose, if the hot tub is making a weird noise, and so on. Your guests are also a great source of information in terms of upkeep.

They will often kindly tell you when something isn't working. Always thank them profusely and send your handyperson over immediately. Guests should never feel that their feedback isn't valued.

For ongoing monthly maintenance items, like landscaping and pest control, choose a day during the month when there is a guest departing, and schedule the vendor to go over to the property directly after checkout. Even if the property is booked for that evening, the maintenance work will be finished in the window between checkout and check-in.

COHOSTING

If you own a property with a partner and you both plan to participate in hosting and guest communication, you'll need to define clear processes and procedures in advance. Set aside some time before your listing goes live to discuss cancellation policies, how you'll handle some of the more common issues, and which partner will be responsible for which tasks. If you plan on managing with your spouse, the policies and procedures need to be even clearer. The last conversation you want to be having at the family dinner table is a disagreement about how one of you responded to a guest.

In my house, it's best if only one of us has the booking platform apps installed at a time. My husband and I have very different communication styles, so if we both look at messages throughout the day, we almost always disagree on how to respond. We find ourselves constantly asking, "Why would you say that? Why did you handle that situation that way?" For us, trading off guest communication duties is the way to go.

If you have a cohost, the best system for the two of you will emerge with time. The most important thing is to make sure that you and your cohost are on the same page when it comes to handling the basics of managing your STR.

Chapter 12

BUILDING WEALTH AND SCALING YOUR PORTFOLIO

Money can't buy you happiness, but it can buy you a yacht big enough to pull right up alongside it.

—DAVID LEE ROTH

Once you get your first STR up and running, you are ready to scale your portfolio. You'll need to define your own goals insofar as how large you want to scale and how fast. What are you working toward: A large multifamily? A mobile home park? A million dollars in cash? Twenty single-family LTR doors? Or maybe you'd like to build an empire of STRs, one in every state? Whatever your goals, you'll need to write them down and display them in a place where you can see them every single day. I write them on a whiteboard in my office. My husband has his written on the bathroom mirror. Some people keep their goals on a Post-it taped to their computer screen. Wherever you place them, the most important thing about your goals is that you have them.

TOP PRIORITY: YOUR CASH RESERVES

Before I get into the "how" of organizing your income from STRs, I am going to spend a fair amount of time on the most important account in your bank: your cash reserves account. As the great Warren Buffett once said, "It's only when the tide goes out that you discover who's been swimming naked."

When the coronavirus shutdowns began happening in March of 2020, STR investors were anxious. We were all expecting to take a big hit, but we had no idea how much of a hit we would take and for how long. There was a lot of talk on STR forums and Facebook groups about how significantly our income would be impacted based on the markets we were invested in. There were a lot of grim predictions and projections floating around. I saw rental arbitragers lose their entire businesses; I saw investors selling off what had previously been lucrative properties at steep discounts in order to feed their families. Many investors whose sole income stream was dependent upon STRs applied for mortgage forbearance on their investments (and probably on their primary homes too) within the first few weeks it was offered. Think about that: A few bad weeks was all that stood between these investors' financial independence and their inability to cover their expenses.

If they'd had sufficient cash reserves in place, they could have held on to their investments and weathered the coronavirus storm, coming out the other side with their very lucrative STR investments intact. But because they did not have the proper cash reserves in place, they almost lost the ability to support their families. Now these investors have to start from scratch. They have to find and purchase new properties, get them ready to rent, and relist them on the booking platforms. This process only extends the length of time they will be without income. Don't be the person who is swimming naked and barely covering their expenses. Set up a cash reserves account, and get it fully funded ASAP.

When the pandemic hit in early 2020, I did not bat an eye (okay, maybe I batted one a little bit), because my cash reserves were built up to withstand zero revenue for the next six months. Luckily, we didn't end up dipping into them at all (thanks to guests who decided to work remotely from our vacation rentals), but had we needed them, they were ready.

Although much of this book is about scaling quickly, it's also true that scaling quickly should not come at the expense of making sure that your current investments have what they need to survive a worst-case scenario. Always keep six months' worth of expenses per property in cash reserves. Expenses include not only utilities but mortgage, property taxes, insurance, and any other upkeep costs. Maintain these cash reserves in a separate bank account. Maybe even remove the cash reserves bank account from your banking dashboard so you don't look at that money every day. The idea is for you to forget it's there so you aren't tempted to spend it.

"But what if a deal comes along that I can't refuse?" you ask. In that case, keep a minimum of three months' worth of expenses tucked away. Six months is ideal, but three will probably be all right in a pinch. In the event that you do dip into the cash reserves bucket in order to make a second real estate purchase, the first account to replenish is your cash reserves account. I cannot stress the importance of a healthy cash reserves account enough—not only in STR investing but in any sort of business, and in life in general. Never work without a net.

FIVE BANK ACCOUNTS FOR SUCCESS

As Mike Michalowicz says, "Profitability isn't an event, it's a habit." (I highly recommend reading his book *Profit First: Transform Your Business from a Cash-Eating Monster to a Money-Making Machine*, if you haven't already). If you maintain the same financial habits over a long period of time, you'll build wealth. I can't tell you what will work best for you, and I'm certainly no CPA, but I can share the system that works for me. In order to get set up, you'll need five bank accounts, one for each of the following:

1. **Revenue.** This is the account the booking platforms will pay your booking revenue into and you'll pay expenses out of.
2. **Taxes.** That 1099 comes in every year, and hopefully yours will continue to grow. However, with big 1099s come big taxes, so make sure this account is set up. Never leave your tax money in your revenue account. That will cause you to think you have more money than you do, which can lead you to spend more than you actually have. Just don't do it.

3. **CapEx.** This is where you'll squirrel away money for the repairs that will inevitably crop up when you least expect them.
4. **Cash reserves.** We talked about your cash reserves account earlier. Think of this as your emergency fund.
5. **Profit.** This is where you'll save money for your next investment.

Next, you'll need to determine what percentage of income you want or need to allocate to each account. That number will differ from investor to investor based on their specific investment goals. If you're planning to scale quickly, you'll allocate less to the cash reserves fund (once that fund reaches at least three months' worth of expenses) and more to the profit fund. If you have an older property in need of maintenance, you'll allocate more to the CapEx fund, and so on. Exactly how you allocate money to your funds will be specific to your property. Nonetheless, here are some basic guidelines:

1. **Taxes:** 30 percent of each booking
2. **CapEx:** 3 percent of each booking
3. **Cash reserves:** 20 percent of each booking until you reach six months' worth of reserves
4. **Profit:** 25 percent of each booking

Allocating funds accordingly will leave you with roughly 22 percent of your earnings in your revenue account, which you'll use to restock items such as paper products and towels and pay your housekeeper, vendors, and utilities. Please understand that these are not hard-and-fast percentages. This is just a template for how to structure your accounts so that every dollar has a place and everything is accounted for.

After reading my list of bank accounts, you may be thinking that the personal bookkeeping required to maintain them is a full-time job in and of itself. Watching for every single deposit to hit your account and then calculating the percentage to transfer to each subsequent account sounds like a lot of work. What if you have multiple properties and receive multiple direct deposits per day? What's the point of automating your STR management only to spend hours every week organizing bank accounts?

It would be very convenient if the major booking platforms allowed for automatic split deposits into multiple accounts, but at the time of this writing, they do not. That's why I've set up my own automated system to move my money around as it comes in. While it may not work for everyone and is certainly not the only way to do things, this system does work. In fact, it works so well that I use it for all my income streams: STR income, real estate sales income, and LTR income.

If you want to implement my automated STR fund allocation system, first you'll need to open accounts with a bank that has a robust digital presence. This system will not work with small local banks and credit unions that do not offer the latest banking technology.

Second, set up the number of accounts necessary to categorize the money you'll be pulling out of each deposit. Maybe you'll need only three; maybe you'll need seven. As explained above, I maintain five accounts (per income stream) with my bank. Periodically, I will add another for a specific project outside of the usual CapEx. You might change the number of accounts as you go, after you figure out which are necessary for you and which aren't. You might like to break down your money into smaller categories than I do. That's totally fine! As long as each account is labeled and makes sense to you, you're doing things right.

Third, you'll need an app that is triggered by a deposit to automatically pull money from the deposit account and distribute funds into the other accounts. I use one called Astra for this. When a deposit hits my account, Astra automatically divvies up the amount based on the percentages I've assigned to each account.

YOUR NEXT DEAL

By utilizing this method, you'll build up enough capital for your next down payment fairly quickly. Then the question becomes: What do I buy next? There are several possibilities, depending on your comfort level.

1. **You could buy another STR in the same market.** Now that you have your systems and processes down, adding another STR asset in the same market as your first makes a lot of sense. In this case, assuming you've already utilized the one 10 percent down vacation home loan you're permitted per market, you'll have to put down 20 percent. However, because you won't have to spend time setting up new systems or securing new vendors in a different market, this approach should give your monthly cash flow a big boost without significantly increasing the amount of work for you.

2. **You can buy another STR in a different market.** This is the second-most-popular choice among the investors I work with because it

requires the least money down. That's because if you move into a new market, you can obtain another 10 percent down vacation home loan.

3. **You can buy a more traditional LTR investment.** A diverse portfolio is never a bad thing. While LTRs won't generally produce as much cash flow as STRs, every investor needs a healthy amount of LTRs in their portfolio. If you've built up your cash flow enough to where it's producing a down payment for a new property quite regularly, it might be a good time to start throwing a few LTR investments into the mix.

VIRTUAL ASSISTANTS

Once you have acquired several STRs and honed your processes to the point that they are streamlined, repeatable, and teachable, it might be time to look into hiring a virtual assistant (VA) to help you with day-to-day tasks. There are a number of companies you can go through to source VAs. Some platforms provide full-time nine-to-five virtual assistants, some offer VAs you can hire by the hour, and some offer a combination of both. VAs can be a great way to offload some of the more menial and tedious tasks related to your business. Heck, my VA even orders my groceries and sends birthday cards for me.

If you're starting to feel squeezed, make a list of the tasks you can easily outsource, or even a list of the tasks you hate to do, and decide which VA option will best suit your needs. After a few months, my VA transformed the way I work. I keep her cc'd on all my emails, and she basically ninjas my whole work life. She knows what kind of support I need before I even have a chance to ask for help. A great VA can be a wonderful addition to your team and an invaluable tool to help grow your business—let your VA support you on your journey toward financial independence.

PARTING WORDS

I have employed each of the strategies in this book to grow my own portfolio, and no matter which option I have chosen, I have never regretted reinvesting my income into real estate. It took me five STRs in the same market to get my cash flow to a point that I could start buying several properties a year without dipping into my other income streams. At that point, my husband and I took a break from buying STRs and went down the LTR path.

We added twenty-three LTR doors (a mix of duplexes and single-family homes) before we came back to STR investing. When we did return, we bought in a new market and took out another 10 percent down vacation home loan. From there, my husband used two 1031 exchanges to sell a couple of our smaller STR units and purchase two larger ones in the same market. For no money out of our own pockets, we went from $300 bookings to $3,000 bookings. Now we are actively looking for ten- to thirty-unit apartment buildings to invest in.

I believe that my personal success with real estate investing can be attributed mostly to adaptability, but also to my belief that STRs are an important asset class in any real estate investment portfolio. I think of my STRs as cash-flow turbochargers within my mixed portfolio of both long- and short-term rentals. When it comes to choosing between the two, the question is not either/or but a matter of which type of investment can best be utilized to propel you down the path toward financial freedom at that given time. I didn't have enough capital to scale as quickly as I wanted using only LTRs. STRs provided the income stream I needed to become the real estate investor I wanted to be and to build generational wealth that I can pass down to my children.

I hope you have found this book helpful. At the very least, I hope you consider it proof that you don't need a huge pile of cash in the bank in order to get started as a real estate investor. If you invest strategically, you can snowball the income from one small STR investment into several STR investments, and several STR investments into as many doors as it takes for you to become financially independent. The difference between becoming a successful investor and never getting started is finding the courage to pull the trigger—so pull the trigger and start your journey to financial freedom with STRs!

"I thought up an ending for it: and he lived happily ever after, till the end of his days."

—J. R. R. TOLKIEN,
THE FELLOWSHIP OF THE RING

ACKNOWLEDGMENTS

To my parents, David and Cindy Allen, thank you for instilling in your children the confidence that has allowed each of us to choose our own path, even if it was something crazy like touring in bands or building a business around buying houses. Everyone deserves the kind of childhood you gave us. I thank you for that, and for the shining example you set for raising my own family. I am truly blessed to have you as parents.

To my sister, Payton, and my brother, Wyatt, thank you for being awesome and supportive.

To Mindy Jensen, thank you for making this book happen.

Katie Miller, Kaylee Walterbach, Savannah Wood, Elizabeth Frels, Wendy Dunning, Louise Collazo, and Taylor Hugo, you're my publishing, marketing, design, and editing wizards! Thank you for the work you put into making this book happen and for putting up with me!

To Brandon Turner, David Greene, and everyone at BiggerPockets: When I first put on my headphones to listen to a podcast about real estate investing, I never dreamed I'd end up building a portfolio and writing a book about it. Thank you for the education you provide for those who dream of something beyond a day job.

To my team at The Short Term Shop, thanks for all the hard work you do to serve our clients!

Special thanks to Pavan & Tracy Mediratta, Julie McCoy, Amity Krause (I could not live without you!), Christy Crowe, the Jerries, Nathan Torgerson, Larry & Stacia Morand, Gennifer Mix, Derek Tellier, Jeana Maddux, Rush Valentine, Paul Sandhu, Share Ross, Sonia Teti, and Che Mendoza for your help along the way.

To all the clients who have ever walked through the door of The Short Term Shop, thank you for allowing us to guide you through your short-term rental investment journey. It's been an honor to serve you and to help you build generational wealth through real estate.

More from
BiggerPockets Publishing

Recession-Proof Real Estate Investing

Take any recession in stride, and never be intimidated by a market shift again. In this book, accomplished investor J Scott dives into the theory of economic cycles and the real-world strategies for harnessing them to your advantage. With clear instructions for every type of investor, this easy-to-follow guide will show you how to make money during all of the market's twists and turns—whether during an economic recession or at any other point in the economic cycle. You'll never look at your real estate business the same way again!

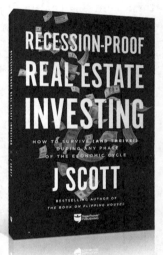

The Book on Advanced Tax Strategies

Saving on taxes means more money for you, your family, and your real estate investments. Learning tax strategies could be the easiest money you ever make! In this comprehensive follow-up to *The Book on Tax Strategies*, best-selling authors and CPAs Amanda Han and Matthew MacFarland bring you more strategies to slash your taxes and turn your real estate investments into a tax-saving machine.

If you enjoyed this book, we hope you'll take a moment to check out some of the other great material BiggerPockets offers. BiggerPockets is the real estate investing social network, marketplace, and information hub, designed to help make you a smarter real estate investor through podcasts, books, blog posts, videos, forums, and more. Sign up today—it's free! **Visit www.BiggerPockets.com.**

The Hands-Off Investor: An Insider's Guide to Investing in Passive Real Estate Syndications

Want to invest in real estate but don't have the time? No matter your level of experience, real estate syndications provide an avenue to invest in real estate without tenants, toilets, or trash—and this comprehensive guide will teach you how to invest in these opportunities the right way. Author Brian Burke, a syndications insider with decades of experience in forming and managing syndication funds, will show you how to evaluate sponsors, opportunities, and offerings so you can pick the right ones and achieve the highest odds of a favorable outcome.

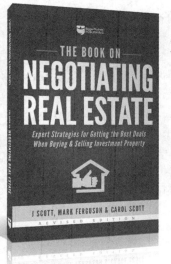

The Book on Negotiating Real Estate

When the real estate market gets hot, it's the investors who know the ins and outs of negotiating who will get the deal. J Scott, Mark Ferguson, and Carol Scott combine real-world experience and the science of negotiation in order to cover all aspects of the negotiation process and maximize your chances of reaching a profitable deal.

More from
BiggerPockets Publishing

Profit Like the Pros: The Best Real Estate Deals Made by Expert Investors

Remarkable real estate deals are happening all around us. Take a look behind the curtain to see exactly how investors have profited from their best deals ever! With twenty-five real-world stories from seasoned investors across the country, this book uncovers the secrets behind unbelievable real estate deals, from sourcing and funding to profiting. Author Ken Corsini—star of HGTV's *Flip or Flop Atlanta*—has distilled his best investor interviews to educate, entertain, and get your wheels spinning.

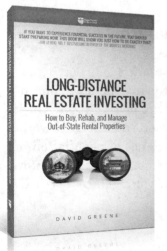

Long-Distance Real Estate Investing

Don't let your location dictate your financial freedom: Live where you want, and invest anywhere it makes sense! The rules, technology, and markets have changed—no longer are you forced to invest only in your backyard. In *Long-Distance Real Estate Investing*, learn an in-depth strategy to build profitable rental portfolios through buying, managing, and flipping out-of-state properties from real estate investor and agent David Greene.

The Book on Tax Strategies for the Savvy Real Estate Investor

Taxes! Boring and irritating, right? Perhaps. But if you want to succeed in real estate, your tax strategy will play a huge role in how fast you grow. A great tax strategy can save you thousands of dollars a year. A bad strategy could land you in legal trouble. With *The Book on Tax Strategies for the Savvy Real Estate Investor*, you'll find ways to deduct more, invest smarter, and pay far less to the IRS!

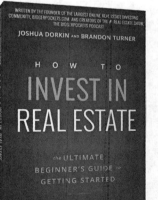

How to Invest in Real Estate

Two of the biggest names in the real estate world teamed up to write the most comprehensive manual ever written on getting started in the lucrative business of real estate investing. Joshua Dorkin and Brandon Turner give you an insider's look at the many different real estate niches and strategies so that you can find which one works best for you, your resources, and your goals.

CONNECT WITH BIGGERPOCKETS

and Become Successful in Your Real Estate Business Today!

Facebook
/BiggerPockets

Instagram
@BiggerPockets

Twitter
@BiggerPockets

LinkedIn
/company/Bigger
Pockets

Website
BiggerPockets.com